EARLY PRAISE

The future will never be the same again. Terence Tse and Mark Esposito have the compelling ability to make sense of the confusing morass of trends and fashions and to map practical routes into the future.

— STUART CRAINER AND DES DEARLOVE, FOUNDERS, THINKERS50

By reading this book, you can be better prepared for what the future could bring.

— NICOLAS PETROVIC, CEO, EUROSTAR INTERNATIONAL

There used to be only two certainties in life: birth and death. Now it would seem there is another and that is change. Understanding the direction and pace of that change can only help us navigate between the previous two certainties. Tse and Esposito's book helps to set us on the right path to navigate through the complex and uncertain future.

— CLIVE NICHOLLS, CEO, UK AND IRELAND, CRAWFORD & COMPANY

This book provides immense insight into megatrends—a topic that is hugely important and relevant for every business leader.

— DIRK KAHL, CFO AND BOARD OF DIRECTORS, LIDL UK GMBH

Brilliantly and accurately explains the artificial intelligence stakes and challenges as well as their impact on business and management. Very insightful and inspiring to think forward and embrace an ever-changing future.

— ESTELLE GIRAUDEAU, MANAGING DIRECTOR, CLUB MED UK AND SCANDINAVIA

In these times of dramatic political, economic, social, and technological change, having an intelligent guide is vital. In this book, Tse and Esposito have created such a guide, helping us navigate our uncertain future.

— GAVIN DEVINE, CEO, NEWGATE COMMUNICATIONS

In the context of today's world, we are global citizens. The DRIVE framework accurately uncovers and highlights the forces shaping us and our surroundings. If we can convince ourselves to study and apply this concept, we can advance on the pathway toward the level of peace, economic stability, as well as social and mental well-being we all strive for.

— CHRISTIAN LEIBL, MANAGING DIRECTOR, HEAD OF CAPITAL STRUCTURE ADVISER, LLOYDS BANKING GROUP

It may not yet come as an "APP," but Tse and Esposito shape a mindset to help DRIVE the future.
— ROGER SPITZ, HEAD OF WEST COAST M & A, BNP PARIBAS

A bold, entertaining, and rich book that gets people to think about what kind of a society we and our children would be facing.
— CHRISTOPHE Y. LE CAILLEC, SVP AND CFO GLOBAL CONSUMER SERVICES, AMERICAN EXPRESS

A book that is indispensable to leaders who want to drive their organizations with strategic foresight.
— PROFESSOR FRANK BOURNOIS, DEAN, ESCP EUROPE BUSINESS SCHOOL

In an age of increasing complexity, it's refreshing to have a compelling and well-thought heuristic to anchor your approach to an ever-changing world. DRIVE is that tool.
— SCOTT EATON, COO, MARKETAXESS EUROPE

2016 caught many by surprise. Tse and Esposito's DRIVE framework is an indispensable tool for leaders to understand megatrends and navigate through the complex and uncertain future.
— PAUL LEE, CEO AND COFOUNDER, AUMEO AUDIO

Tse and Esposito's framework helps to clarify how megatrends will shape the future of business but also focuses the mind of executives on key questions that need to be dealt with today.
— MARC BARONE, MANAGING DIRECTOR, WATER UK & IRELAND, AECOM

Tse and Esposito have provided us with a valuable addition to the art of foresight for the era of volatilities and accelerations. We cannot get enough inspiration to see today's little signs of tomorrow's big change.

— OLAF J. GROTH, PHD, PROFESSOR OF GLOBAL STRATEGY, INNOVATION, AND ECONOMICS, AND PROGRAM DIRECTOR FOR DIGITAL FUTURES, HULT INTERNATIONAL BUSINESS SCHOOL; MANAGING DIRECTOR, EMERGENT FRONTIERS GROUP

This book is a great testament on how scholars and academia can contribute with a global compass on how to face and embrace the most daunting challenges of our times. The DRIVE framework is an absolute required tool for all those executives who want to make a difference.

— LOICK ROCHE, PHD, DEAN AND CEO, GRENOBLE ÉCOLE DE MANAGEMENT

Terence Tse and Mark Esposito are not only brilliant thinkers. Their research insights are practical and actionable, generating real value to their readers. This is a must-read in a fast-changing world.

— MARCOS VAENA, CHIEF, SECTOR AND ENTERPRISE COMPETITIVENESS, INTERNATIONAL TRADE CENTER

As a business strategist, I plan for the future like I play chess, trying to predict what other moves will take place and prepare accordingly. This book is a must for all those in business who wish to continue to win against the future's uncertain game plan.

— J. C. REYES, LEAD CONSULTANT, EFFICIENCY.CA

This is the book to read to get clarity of the current state of play.
— FRANCESCO RATTALINO, PHD, MANAGING DIRECTOR
AND PROFESSOR, ESCP EUROPE TURIN CAMPUS

Understanding future trends is not just an intellectual exercise. It is much more than this. Vis-à-vis the acceleration of change processes, driven mainly by technology, thinking clearly about the future has become a vital necessity, which could represent a company's ability to survive and thrive in the market. Terence Tse and Mark Esposito's book looks at the most relevant forthcoming changes and equips decision makers with a valuable framework to manage the threats ahead of our time.
— ENRICO SASSOON, EDITOR IN CHIEF,
HARVARD BUSINESS REVIEW ITALIA

Kodak, BlackBerry, Blockbuster, and Encyclopædia Britannica didn't see what hit them. Ignore megatrends at your peril. Tse and Esposito link current megatrends to what it means for you so you can harness change rather than become its next victim.
— NICOLAS GRANT, CEO, SEVERN TRENT
SERVICES, UK, IRELAND, AND ITALY

In an ever-increasing fast-paced world, megatrends are essential to deliver breakthrough strategies and enduring performance. Tse and Esposito are setting us on the right path to navigate through a complex and uncertain future.
— RAPHAEL MIOLANE, CEO, PIZZA HUT UK & IRELAND

Thought provoking and very topical in the current socioeconomic and political climate. This book provides a user-friendly framework to help readers gain perspective of current events in the context of wider trends and to consider how a variety of seemingly unconnected events might be the start of the next megatrend. Highly recommended.

— GAVIN WEIR, PARTNER, CORPORATE/M
& A PRACTICE, WHITE & CASE LLP

With this outstanding book, Terence and Mark will empower people to think about the "now" and the "next" with the same degree of confidence, by making them connect the dots between actions and reactions.

— DANIELA BIAGI, GROUP HEAD OF THE ACADEMY,
LONDON STOCK EXCHANGE GROUP

The only certainty is that there is no certainty. This book takes a fascinating look at the complexity of the future through the megatrends driving the ever-accelerating pace of change. Whether leading yourself, others, or organizations, you will find this book an invaluable guide to navigating today's massive transformative changes. It will help you to thrive and not just survive. I could not put this book down.

— GEORGE KOHLRIESER, PHD, PROFESSOR OF LEADERSHIP
AND ORGANIZATIONAL BEHAVIOR, IMD

UNDERSTANDING HOW THE FUTURE UNFOLDS

UNDERSTANDING HOW THE FUTURE UNFOLDS

Using DRIVE to Harness the Power of Today's Megatrends

INEQUALITIES
VOLATILITY, SCALE AND COMPLEXITY
RESOURCE SCARCITY
DEMOGRAPHIC & SOCIAL CHANGES
ENTERPRISING DYNAMICS

TERENCE C. M. TSE PHD
& MARK ESPOSITO PHD

COPYRIGHT © 2017 TERENCE C.M. TSE & MARK ESPOSITO
All rights reserved.

UNDERSTANDING HOW THE FUTURE UNFOLDS
Using DRIVE to Harness the
Power of Today's Megatrends

ISBN 978-1-61961-554-0 *Paperback*
      978-1-61961-555-7 *Ebook*

TERENCE'S DEDICATION:

To my wife, Céline, and children, Clélia and Lucile.

MARK'S DEDICATION:

To the "chancletos," aka my pack: Alina, Kendra, and Frappy. Your presence is a daily blessing.

CONTENTS

FOREWORD 17
INTRODUCTION 21

PART 1: UNDERSTANDING MEGATRENDS
1. WHY MEGATRENDS MATTER 39
2. WHAT IS THE DRIVE FRAMEWORK? 59

PART 2: THE REALITY OF TODAY
3. D: DEMOGRAPHIC AND SOCIAL CHANGES ... 79
4. R: RESOURCE SCARCITY 105
5. I: INEQUALITIES 129

PART 3: HARNESSING THE POWER OF HOPE
6. V: VOLATILITY, SCALE, AND COMPLEXITY ... 169
7. E: ENTERPRISING DYNAMICS 201

CONCLUSION 223
ABOUT THE AUTHORS 229

TR MEGA NDS

FOREWORD

BY XAVIER ROLET

The first time I met Terence Tse was in January 2016 when he interviewed me on the topic of megatrends that he and his colleague, Mark Esposito, had started to identify. The conversation ultimately led to an article that we coauthored on capital inequality—the preference for debt over share equity in UK and European capital raising, consequently denying innovative, high-growth companies the type of finance they require to invest, grow, and create the jobs of the future.

Since then, we have noted several significant events around the world, some of which followed an unexpected path that resulted in major geopolitical and macroeconomic consequences: positive or negative depending on your standpoint but consequences all the same.

One thing is for certain, the ride ahead will be just as bumpy, if not more so, and it is always hard to predict exactly where we are heading. This ride is akin to venturing into a choppy sea in the middle of the night. We are constantly trying to see and plan for rocks on the horizon—and this book metaphorically aims to turn the light on in the lighthouse.

Using their framework, DRIVE, the authors want to develop their foresight by looking at people, resources, social equality, technological changes, and events, as well as new business models and innovations—all of which inform the foundations and workings of modern society.

As the book examines each of these in detail, readers are promised insight and inspiration into what can be expected in the future and how they can prepare themselves for the possibility of new realities. The authors have drawn their views from a wide range of sources. They've assimilated the ideas of other thinkers, students, corporate executives, and entrepreneurs, as well as interviewed experts from the World Economic Forum, the International Trade Center, and the European Union.

Perhaps the greatest insight from this book is that as much as there are challenges that governments, societies, and businesses have to overcome in the near future and beyond, there are just as many opportunities ahead for making the world a better place. This work boldly offers a road map for those wishing to navigate through the seemingly unpredictable future.

You are about to go on an incredible journey—a journey that is not just fascinating but also full of inspiring stories. This is a great way to start exploring the future. See you there!

— XAVIER ROLET, KBE
CEO, LONDON STOCK EXCHANGE GROUP

INTRODUCTION

A FRAMEWORK FOR THE FUTURE

We're proud to be outcasts in the academic world. You wouldn't guess it from looking at our résumés or degrees. For most of our careers, we've been developing our own ideas, concepts, and frameworks for looking at the world and teaching in accordance with them, and most importantly, we never hid in the ivory tower. We left it a long time ago.

Indeed, the principles, ideas, and frameworks that emerge from conventional academia don't adhere neatly to what we consider our jobs as educators should be. Our frustration is that the pace of change in the new global economy is moving so fast, we find that many of the existing frameworks, as well as entire subjects, have failed to catch up.

As advisers, commentators, speakers, and professors of finance and economic strategy, we're often invited to comment on global economic occurrences, as was the case in 2008. At the height of the financial crisis, a prominent bank asked Terence to run a workshop to help the senior management team understand the origin of the crisis. The inquiry stopped him in his tracks. He thought, *Why would a banker not have a solid grasp on all the factors that contributed to the collapse of the banking system?*

It turned out the bank employees didn't have the first clue. It was in the same boat as many of the other experts and professionals in their fields: lacking the ability or the tools to connect the dots. Most people are not able to see the fundamental connectivity between world events. Activities or occurrences that may appear completely unrelated on the surface are, in fact, interwoven when you scratch the surface. The banking crisis of 2008 is just one indicator of the interconnectedness of world events, albeit a significant one. Any event of significance, these days, is equally part of a great order of connected factors, often unseen by the traditional logic of things.

With the intention of helping executives understand

the complex and rapidly changing drivers of the global economy, we developed some time ago a course called Business 360. We wanted to incorporate multiple business disciplines and merge them into one holistic viewpoint. The central idea behind Business 360 was to provide a comprehensive perspective of the business climate today to better prepare for tomorrow. Our goal was to help executives be more effective analytical managers.

As the Business 360 course evolved, we found ourselves increasingly focusing on megatrends—initially through assignments for our students and later as an anchor for all of our discussions. Megatrends are big changes that affect governments, economies, societies, and cultures over the near and long-term. These are the fundamental forces that have started to dramatically shape the social, economic, and political landscapes of tomorrow's world. At times, these trends clash with one another; other times, they go hand in hand. Little by little, we noticed certain megatrends served as the glue that linked everything we'd been discussing and wrestling with for years.

The framework we had been looking for existed in the world all around us. We realized—accidentally—our best field of research and the most pertinent tool for analysis was right in front of our eyes. Everything we read in the headlines, saw on the news, and experienced firsthand in everyday activities fed into our evolving framework. We refer to that framework by the acronym DRIVE, which represents five megatrends: demographic and social changes; resource scarcity; inequalities; volatility, scale, complexity; and enterprising dynamics—all of which inspired this book.

D: Demographic and social changes. The focus is on people, because people are at the center of all our activities.

R: Resource scarcity. All human activities require some input to create output, which is how we advance.

I: Inequalities. This trend focuses on how resources and output are (poorly) allocated and distributed.

V: Volatility, scale, and complexity. Volatility relates to the external environment along with the means and scale of change, or how change can improve the future.

E: Enterprising dynamics. This relates to business and how varied technologies or advances will be used and what impact they will have. It also refers to the business models emerging from around the world.

The increasing pace of various factors throughout the world, all of which we'll discuss in depth within these pages, became the foundation of our approach. Much has been written about trends and what the future holds. Our orchestrated effort to connect the dots into a unique framework provides a fresh perspective. We're not fortune-tellers with crystal balls. Ours is not a prescriptive 1-2-3-4 formula for looking at the world. Rather, DRIVE allows people to move fluidly from one key growth area to the next while generating their own understanding and application of each.

Things are happening at an ever-faster rate. The world's operating system is being rebooted with increasing frequency, if not being constantly rewritten. To survive in today's global economic climate and prepare for tomorrow, it is imperative to have an understanding of:

1. What is happening from multiple perspectives
2. How things are connected

The DRIVE framework brings it all together. It focuses on five key interrelated perspectives that impact our lives, and it offers a new way of thinking about the future. Inside this book, we'll dissect each of the components in detail and provide the context for which to use them when identifying new opportunities.

TODAY VERSUS TOMORROW

We are living in a tremendously uncertain world. Often, we can only guess what will happen down the road. Nevertheless, to survive, business owners try to anticipate potential future events and behaviors with a highly strategic mindset. They ask the following: Where is the market heading? How will that impact my company? Where is capital going? How can I make my business prosper, despite this volatility in the markets? What products will people buy one, five, fifteen, or fifty years from now? Is climate change a real threat to my business? Many business owners and CEOs feel confined or restrained by outdated models that don't allow much room to pivot or grow in new directions.

For example, executives in the insurance industry are looking for ways to appeal to existing and future generations of insureds. Auto insurance faces multiple challenges, especially as innovation accelerates around autonomous vehicles. "Who is responsible for the insurance if individuals are no longer 'in the driver's seat'? Is it the car owner, the 'driver,' the software manufacturer, the remote IT operating company, the car manufacturer, or some combination thereof? Instead of covering accidents due to the drivers, will it cover accidents due to software failure or cyberbreaches?" asked Adam Winslow, UK CEO of AIG Life, a global insurance company.[1]

It's likely the engineers working on the development of driverless cars are not thinking about the auto insurance industry. They're thinking about the new product, and how to make it safe, affordable, and marketable. Rest assured, however, the auto insurers *are* thinking about the industry and how driverless cars will impact their business, their viability, and their pocketbooks. As the world races ahead, who will be left behind and why?

We tend to think that today is certain and tomorrow is uncertain, but that logic needs to be flipped. Certainty, the present implies there is nothing we can do today to alter an outcome, and yet, we *can* make changes for the better today. Uncertainty implies we can have a different and hopefully better future. The better we deal with our current problems, the higher our chances are of creating a better future. If we don't act now, tomorrow will not improve. Understanding where we are going helps us understand where we are currently.

Each of the megatrends we discuss in DRIVE is a trajectory that will fulfill its course over time. If we look at a current phenomenon, we know it will follow a certain evolution.

---

[1] Interview with Adam Winslow, March 3, 2016.

For example, demographic and social changes—we know the global population is aging, and as time goes on, there will be more old people in society than there will be children. If we don't do anything, the future of that trajectory is certain. We're trying to identify areas today that have the greatest degree of uncertainty. If we can change the trajectory, we can change the future.

Our view is different than most, which tends to think of the future as "out there." People think if they don't know what the future looks like, they can't control it. Effectively, they're allowing their destiny to control the present, which is a passive mentality, if not downright defeatist.

We advocate for a more proactive approach. If you want to change the future, all you need to do is look at today's events. Then imagine how these events will deploy over time. The future is nothing more than an evolution of trends that are currently unfolding. We're still in the driver's seat, and we can take steps "now" for a better "next." We want to empower people to think about today *and* tomorrow with the same degree of confidence, because they are not mutually exclusive. If we try today to deal with the widening inequalities, we ought to arrive at a better society tomorrow.

DRIVE is an effective means for business executives,

entrepreneurs, and scholars to connect the dots between actions and reactions. The five megatrends within DRIVE provide a new lens through which to view current events to make better decisions and identify opportunities.

COMPLEXITY AND THE HUMAN CONDITION

In many ways, we're lucky. We could think about world events from a fresh perspective *before* circumstances and events go completely berserk. *Now* is precisely the right time to ask ourselves what sort of impact our behaviors, attitudes, practices, and assumptions will have on a larger scale.

We don't think about simplifying the complexity that today's business owners face but rather, clarifying the complexity. There are undoubtedly blind spots and gray areas on the horizon. Instead of pretending they don't exist, or they're beyond our control, we'll shine a light on them, so they can be more effectively addressed and overcome. When people start thinking about how things are connected and what the implications of those relationships are, the desire to run and hide is removed. The complexity in and of itself is not the problem; however, the traditional approach to it no longer holds water.

Most people regard the future in the same way a child

fears a monster hiding in the dark. When you can't see what's in front of you, or what's lurking in the shadows, you conjure all kinds of evils—real or imagined. All you need is a torch to illuminate the way, and you realize it's not as bad as you imagined. You need to get through the darkness and open the door to make sense of what's in the room.

Knowing the answer seems to be more important than ever. Consider the so-called Overton Window—created by John Overton, a libertarian think tanker, who suggested that an idea that falls outside the political mainstream, even though it is "radical" or even "unthinkable," can become acceptable once stated and argued for, framed, and restated. Once something (or someone) is introduced, intangible as it may seem at the time, it gradually works its way into the collective internal psyche.[2]

For example, there was a call for a referendum on the membership of the European Union (EU) in 1997. Ridiculous as it sounded back then, it became a possibility, and then before we knew it, a reality.[3] To a certain extent, Trump's victory can be partially attributed to his bringing in the political impossibilities.[4] Ignorance is not bliss.

2   http://www.mackinac.org/12887
3   http://www.lrb.co.uk/v38/n15/john-lanchester/brexit-blues
4   http://www.nationalreview.com/article/428200/donald-trump-overton-window-american-political-debate

Fear of the unknown and the shifts in Overton Window are not the only challenges we face. Due in large part to advances in technology, humans have shorter attention spans than goldfish,[5] and we tend to focus exclusively on the things that pertain directly to us. People very often direct their limited attention to matters at hand or the immediate operating environments. Other things that happen in the world are not as immediately relevant. Even though there may be a relationship to the banking industry, we focus on what we can understand and what directly relates to us. Anything outside of our line of focus does not benefit from our time, interest, consideration, and sadly, attention. When Mark talked about the blockchain technology in a workshop for a major international bank, he was surprised that none of the senior executives among the participants had ever heard of it. Yet, the very same bank has published an extensive report discussing how the technology can revolutionize the industry.

It is important to tune in to what is happening around us, not just the immediate but the wider surrounding. One of the greatest paradoxes of the connected world is that many people are gradually losing their interest to connect to the outside, thereby losing the ability to make sense of the reality and becoming alienated by the pace of events.

---

5   http://www.telegraph.co.uk/science/2016/03/12/humans-have-shorter-attention-span-than-goldfish-thanks-to-smart/

THE DRIVE MINDSET

The business world, as it is currently structured, rewards both short-termism and specialization. There's nothing necessarily wrong with either of those tendencies. However, an unwillingness to take new factors or developments into account can become a liability. The DRIVE framework allows for a broader view. It invites people to take various factors that they have previously never considered into account and dissect certain variables from a new angle.

Opportunities are a direct consequence of how megatrends shape our societies. For example, as people move from the countryside into the cities, opportunities are created as people struggle to find space in an urban setting. The population is mobile, and that mobility also creates opportunity. Regardless of what expert economic analysts support, DRIVE emulates the real market economy, every day, whether you're looking at demographic and social changes, resource scarcity, inequalities, volatility (scale and complexity), or enterprising dynamics.

When we are able to understand the relationship among these elements, we're able to go deeper into what we call a first-order effect. We're able to understand that society is truly evolving, and evolution is a breeding ground for business opportunities. Several things happening at once then lead us to a second order, or cause and effect, and so forth. The effect spreads out like a giant ripple. It's like the movie *Inception*, where Leonardo DiCaprio experiences multiple layers of complexity within the same dream. Opportunities arise within every single wrinkle of the inception, but they change radically, depending on your ability to go deeper in the analysis.

Education teaches us to think in terms of fixed structures and silos. We've found the more educated people are, the less they are able to see the interrelatedness between events. "Schools," in the words of education researcher Sugata Mitra, "are a machine built by the British Empire to produce the people needed to run bureaucratic administrative activities."[6] This is still pretty much with us today. Curriculum, from children to postgraduate, often favors processing things rather than building them; it often gives preference to force-feeding knowledge over raising curiosity. No wonder unspecialized people are often more skilled in seeing the big picture because without restriction, they can think more fluidly.

We recognize that people will take what they want from the information in this book. We are not in a position to tell anyone how to think, although we hope to get them to

---

6   https://www.ted.com/talks/sugata_mitra_build_a_school_in_the_cloud/transcript?language=en#t-113512

think and to think aloud. As educators, we know everyone walks out of the classroom with a different spin on what was presented there, even when specific instructions are provided. Some people, despite our protestations, will see this as a forecasting book. That is a nuance of the material and topics we will discuss in depth in the next chapter.

The real opportunity within DRIVE is to allow ideas to flow more freely. It's not a tool kit but rather a mindset that requires nothing more than a willingness to think differently. For businesses and entrepreneurs, it offers inspiration to change the way you think about your own capabilities. Yes, we ask big questions, but we've seen people discover they had the answers inside of themselves all along. They simply were not looking at the information from a broad perspective.

For students and the younger generation, this book may give you a hint as to what lies ahead in the economy and society that you can be living in. Starting to think today about what can affect tomorrow allows you to anticipate new opportunities and to respond faster to new changes. As some of our mentors taught us along the way, forewarned is forearmed, as they say. We genuinely hope to service youth by providing them with some food for thought.

If you're frustrated by sitting in the same traffic jam every day at 8:05 a.m., you might have a different take on your predicament if you understood the influx of people from the country to the cities. Adopting a more global view alleviates some of the burden and gets the wheels turning.

For example, why are there so many people in their cars at 8:05 a.m.? Where did these people come from, and where are they going? How can the infrastructure within the city be improved to accommodate this influx of people? Will they widen the roads or increase public transportation? Will someone build a coffee shop at the intersection to capture all of these thirsty and hungry commuters? What devices or technologies could be used in the car to increase the productivity of the morning commute? How are the emissions impacting the air quality? This line of questioning can go on almost indefinitely. It's necessary to follow the question trail to better understand how something as simple and mundane as morning traffic relates to multiple, larger considerations, and ultimately, opportunities. And finally, am I able to understand that as frustrating as it may be, I am "traffic" myself, even if stuck in it?

Our goal is to empower people to make these sorts of connections themselves. It's not about us, or what we're sharing; it's about people utilizing a framework to get to their own aha moment. We're simply trying to help refine a thought process to arrive at deeper conclusions faster, in such a way that the conclusions do not manifest in an aha moment at all. Rather, the mindset we're proposing is internalized and realizations come quietly from within. The fact is, we're not teaching anyone anything new. We're showing them how to make connections, and in doing so, overcome problems.

Whenever we present DRIVE to new people, whether family, friends, students, colleagues, businesses, or policy makers, it's always met with fresh enthusiasm, because the context is applicable consistently and immediately. No matter what's happening in the economic, environmental, political, or social headlines, DRIVE applies. Understanding DRIVE simply gives the event a new nuance with which to look forward. We're excited to share the framework here, because it's a different way to think about the future, it's comprehensive, and it's universal. You control the GPS. Now go, DRIVE.

PART 1

UNDERSTANDING MEGATRENDS

CHAPTER 1
WHY MEGATRENDS MATTER

—

A megatrend is a trend that has universal impact. Regardless of where you live or your economic status, megatrends affect everyone and everything as a society, as an environment, and as a planet. They represent patterns or changes with disruptive forces that take place over an extended period, often decades, and create major changes for business and society as a whole. Megatrends have sufficient energy and strength to launch specific trajectories. They move everything in a certain direction.

Each of the five megatrends we discuss in DRIVE—demographic and social changes, resource scarcity, inequalities, volatility (scale and complexity), and enterprising dynamics—has its own distinct course of action. Regarding demographic and social changes, there's a clear and consistent story across the globe: the population in many parts of the world is getting older, and there are fewer young people. Resources are becoming scarce. Inequality is widening between the rich and the poor, to the degree that inequality is now a global issue. Due to the increasing scale, complexity, and speed of digitization and automations, volatility manifests in the disruption that has become business as usual. The use of technologies to find new ways of engaging customers as well as enhancing the running in the backend has given rise to new enterprising dynamics across companies of all sizes, industries, and markets.

Megatrends matter more now than they ever have before. The world is a global collective entity, although we don't yet have the psychology for it. We tend to think on a local level: our daily tasks, individual career paths, the people around us, the organization we work for, and so forth. However, on a global level, there is increased connectivity. The Internet links all of humanity—across countries, oceans, and languages—to the degree that technology and the integrated trends are the new organizational structure of the world. In a generic sense, the life someone lives in Africa more closely resembles the life someone lives in the Midwestern region of the United States today than it did fifty years ago. The lines have become blurred, and the trends are globally converging.

Nevertheless, when we talk about macroeconomics, especially in the classroom, there is a limit to how much it can tell us. For example, if we said, "The GDP of China is expected to grow at 7 percent this year," we know that the fundamentals of the economy appear to be functioning. But what do we know beyond that? What does that level of data tell us about what is going on with the GDP or the economic state of the country? How do we differentiate that growth from positive (more schools, more health care) to negative (more pollution, more "white elephant" projects, more vacant office blocks built)? It is interesting to know what the data is, but to understand what it means in the big picture, we need to go deeper.

Many people are not able to make the connection between economic data and understanding how the economy works or what it means for them. If you're running a business and read the statistic about the GDP, you'd likely think, *Hey, that's great. But what does it have to do with me?* If you are still unconvinced, ask yourself this: "How can quantitative easing impact your life?" Macroeconomics is an exciting topic. There are whole schools of people, theorists, and scholars who eat, sleep, and breathe it, but it's not directly relatable or relevant to *most* people. This is where megatrends come in.

Megatrends are the undercurrents that drive where we are going. If we were going down a river in a boat, the megatrends would be the currents that carry us along. Macroeconomics is more like the wind, the temperature, or the sky. If the weather is bad, the currents will be affected, just as they would if the weather is favorable. What carries us from one point to another is the river itself. We like to think of megatrends in the same way. The water in the river is a physical entity. You can reach your hand over the side of the boat and feel it. The sky is much harder to touch, because it's an abstract concept.

WHY MEGATRENDS MATTER FOR BUSINESS

In the 1980s, good business meant being physically present in the marketplace. You had an idea or a business proposition, you found a location, opened your business, worked hard, sold your product, and eventually people recognized it (or not). You kept on working hard to get recognized within your market space. The business model started on the inside with the idea, and worked its way out into the world. Inside/out was the behavior that constituted "business as normal."

Yesterday's business model does not apply today. Unless you're in a closed market without any competition, the old "build it first and then they will come" strategy is yesterday's news. What drives opportunities and sales in today's business world is the ability of a company to capture nuances. Success is directly related to how people feel about a product or a brand and how that product or brand makes you feel about yourself. How do you talk about it and use it? Who are you talking to about it and where? Do you discuss it at the coffee shop, in the gym, around the water cooler, or online through social media? Today's business world is driven outside/in.

Understanding the world around us and looking at it through a scope of growth, is, in our view, the best way to identify new business opportunities. This perspective allows you to better recognize what products or services will sell. The product itself may not be the next "sure thing," but perhaps it is positioned in a way that makes people feel good about themselves. It depends largely on your market. Some product markets demand immediate access, speed, or personalization. The opportunity for specialization and variance is vast, but understanding megatrends gives business owners a language that leads to better research and development in the field.

Business schools often give students straightforward,

early exercises such as, "Go home and map out the strategy you think best suits your idea." Or, "Come up with the solution as to how the protagonist in the case can solve the problem faced." Most of what we see in class are models or model ideas that will work just fine—for now. The students assess the current business landscape and situations, and then they dutifully make their idea fit into the prescribed circumstances. It's not necessarily sustainable or scalable, but they've done the assignment and checked it off the list.

However, things get far more interesting when someone takes something that could happen in the future into account. When we look ahead and analyze the strength or longevity of an idea from that perspective, we are able to have a more valuable discussion about long-term strategy and viability. The job of being a CEO is much harder these days than any time in the past. This is because, said Patrick Martell, CEO of Informa Business Intelligence, "The business environment continues to change. CEOs have to make business decisions within a much shorter window and without necessarily having the benefit of analysis and hard facts. Despite the *E* in CEO, it is no longer about executive decisions; it is about learning and thinking about technologies, cultures, and people. Market and customer insights are critical to business planning and gaining a competitive edge."[1]

Scott Eaton, COO of MarketAxess Europe, which provides institutional investors and global dealers with advanced e-trading capabilities, further adds, "In a business landscape that is dominated by rapid technological change, it is not just about understanding how technologies work. What's far more important is to understand how technologies interact with businesses and societies, as well as how business and social evolutions are impacting technologies. We should be questioning the assumptions we have today and sensing what could be taking place ahead of us. We benefit a great deal from looking at the future trends."[2] We could not agree with them more. We are at a point in time right now where *not* taking megatrends into account when forecasting business ideas is actually dangerous. Let's look briefly at each of the five megatrends within DRIVE and assess what might happen if they were ignored.

For demographic and social changes, what would happen if none of the governments in the world were able to support the multiple and varied needs of senior citizens, who are increasing in number and living longer? If we don't start thinking about the future and what it could look like

---

[1] Interview with Patrick Martell, March 24, 2016.
[2] Interview with Scott Eaton, April 14, 2016.

for this population of people, we will easily face a pension crisis. In fact, the matter is so pressing that many people are already talking about it. Hopefully, they have devised a plan to alleviate some of the financial, logistical, and even emotional toll an impending pension crisis would entail.

Likewise, the issue of resource scarcity becomes dire when we stop to think about it. As online retail continues to thrive, the waste generated from these shipments will not only use up more resources but also create a significant amount of waste.[3] What kind of future are we looking at if we continue to rely on more and more processed foods? What impact will that have on the obesity epidemic, and how will people afford the rising costs of health care? What impact will rising health-care costs have on people's disposable income and how they spend it?

Similarly, if we don't step in to address widening inequalities, at what point will the world stop being divided into two imbalanced classes: the haves and the have-nots? Are the older generations benefiting at the expense of the younger ones? How much should we allow automation and artificial intelligence to replace the human workforce? *D*, *R*, and *I* are the gravest of the megatrends, because if

---

3   Man Zhang, Yaning Chen, and Yanjun Shen, "China's Environmental Threats of Internet Shopping Packaging Wastes," *Journal of Environmental & Analytical Toxicology* 6, no. 5 (2016), doi: 10.4172/2161-0525.1000401.

we don't start thinking about them now, we may be too late to find a solution.

Volatility, scale, complexity, and enterprising dynamics represent emerging businesses, business models, and ideas. At the same time, digitization, automation, robotics, and artificial intelligence are gobbling up blue- and white-collar workers alike. They offer hope for tomorrow because through innovation, we are able to do things and be in places and know things that were previously impossible. Companies without direct access to capital can now raise money through crowdsourcing and other fund-raising methods—a phenomenon deemed impossible even ten years ago. With advanced technological data, we are now able to pinpoint precise areas where an epidemic is occurring in real time. Combining this with cloud technologies, on-the-spot diagnostics lead to faster and more accurate results, which means faster response to and even the prevention of epidemics.

Understanding megatrends is a competitive necessity. If we don't grasp the trends, we'll have a hard time making sense of what is happening in the world around us. We can no longer rely on an analysis of the past to forecast what the next few months or years will be like.

People love to arm themselves with data. They think

the more information they have, the more accurate they will be when trying to pinpoint future performance. An entire generation of salespeople grew up analyzing sales patterns from previous months to determine their key performance indicators and objectives for current and future sales cycles. The system worked well for some time, but now, that approach does not yield the same results. A lot of salespeople are standing around scratching their heads trying to figure out why their sales are plummeting despite the forecast.

What's missing is the desire to understand *why* sales plunged in a particular month. Spikes and dips are nothing more than the evolution of the trends within our society. It stands to reason that we should be using a model that looks at trends in order to determine the next best action, so we can adjust.

We're not saying we can predict the future or even that anyone should try. We simply want our readers to become more engaged and aware of what is happening around them. Our hope is that by reading this book, you will become more attuned to events and how they are connected so they can update your own viewpoints on a continual basis. Philip Tetlock, an expert in forecasting, points out that the critical ingredient of real foresight (and not just forecast) is the style of thinking and not just in-depth knowledge. Such thinking involves looking at any issue from multiple perspectives and continuously taking in new information to refine the views.[4] We believe our framework, DRIVE, can offer additional perspectives to our readers.

CAUSE AND EFFECT

A few months before this book was published, the Brexit referendum was voted on in the UK. Terence lives and teaches in London, and we are both scholars and educators of international economic policy and finance. The vote was equivalent to a tsunami in our respective worlds.

Personal opinion notwithstanding, the vote made waves the world over, but nowhere as strong as in the UK. The media reported a significant rise in anti-immigrant hate crimes throughout the country,[5] many as a direct result of the referendum. The media screamed, "Brexit is the cause of hate crimes." The same happened in the United States with the 2016 presidential election.

Brexit is emblematic of the divide between people, but

---

4   Philip Tetlock and Dan Gardner, *Superforecasting: The Art & Science of Prediction* (New York: Random House, 2015).
5   http://www.independent.co.uk/news/uk/crime/brexit-hate-crime-racism-immigration-eu-referendum-result-what-it-means-eurospectic-areas-a7165056.html

what was happening *before* the vote that pointed to this? When you look at the specific undercurrents, you'll notice distinct inequalities between people living in cities like London or Manchester and people living in the northern part of the country. Most people attribute the rise in racial aggression to a single event, yet inequalities are the sources of motivation.

This example can be applied to a wide variety of circumstances throughout the world. Events do not occur in a vacuum. As educators, we are always sensitive to cause and effect. However, the trends show us that causes are much more important for us to understand than the effects per se. Think about the event as the very tip of an iceberg, the clear majority of which is hidden beneath the water. Trends help us to study what lies below the surface instead of focusing exclusively on what we can easily see. The actual event(s) carries/carry little significance when weighed against all the other events that led up to it.

Economists say, "Correlation is not causation." We know certain variables are related, but we don't know why. The same can be said of causation versus causality. We know there is a cause and effect, but if we don't look at events over a given period, the relationship between those events has little meaning. Megatrends behave the same way. Nothing happens overnight. When you expand the time line of analysis, you better understand what is really happening and why.

For example, when Obama took office in 2009, the United States faced one of the highest unemployment rates in its history. Many among the population and the media pointed their fingers at Obama's new administration as the single event responsible for the unemployment rate.

The fact is, about twenty years before Obama took office, the United States began dismantling the manufacturing arm of the workforce and moving the bulk of the work overseas. It was much cheaper at the time to produce goods in China than it was to produce them at home in the United States. The decision to pursue cheap labor in the 1990s was responsible for the high unemployment rate at the beginning of the Obama administration. The administration itself was not the cause of unemployment, just as the Brexit referendum was not the cause of the rise in hate crimes in the UK. As a species, we have limited availability to see connections and even less ability to think in terms of unintended consequences.

INCREASED CONNECTIONS, BLURRING BOUNDARIES

Many of the dynamics that we perceive today are nothing

more than the unfolding of events that have been developing little by little over the last twenty or even fifty years. A colleague recently remarked, "The price of globalization that we see today was never fully integrated in our lives, but it has been a developing facade." What he meant was, we haven't really become global. We have become accustomed to products produced through a global supply chain, and we travel with relative ease around the map, but we haven't changed the way we think about value in a global manner. We have failed to identify the inherent connections and causalities, so we overlook most of the intelligence.

Consider what happened to Kodak, the photography giant. The company failed, because it did not see the future coming. It became too complacent with the old "tried and true" and remained focused on print photography while the rest of the world marched toward digitization. It had a disorganized response to change. By the time it woke up to the trend, it had been left behind. Eventually, Kodak was able to recover from bankruptcy and devastation but never to the grandeur it once knew. Sticking to clear demarcation has cut off many possible connections.

We tend to think of industry in categories: computer, photo, insurance, or automotive. In today's world, companies cannot afford to pigeonhole themselves into a single core competency. They cannot excuse themselves from the conversation happening all around them, or they are at risk. Failure doesn't come from what you know; it comes from what you ignore. Exposure is the best antidote.

Traditional industry boundaries are disappearing. Conventional competitor analyses are swiftly losing their value and merit. Businesses need to build capacity for tomorrow by engaging in what is going on today. A company is never "done" innovating, pivoting, or growing unless, of course, it fails to adapt to the times.

Nicolas Petrovic, CEO of Eurostar, perhaps best sums up the importance of jettisoning the traditional concept of boundaries. "We are not a train business. We are not even a transport business. We are, first and foremost, a social experience company." This is partly because many of the customers are no longer bound by traditional boundaries. "They have an international outlook. They don't see borders. These travelers have a very different mental map," Petrovic added.[6]

Skype is another example of a company that stepped outside of the box to fill a need. They are not a phone company, but they provide phone services, for free, through the Internet. How do you think the phone companies feel

---

6 Interview with Nicolas Petrovic, October 28, 2016.

about Skype? Not very good. We do our banking through our mobile phones. Energy is transmitted through solar panels without going through an energy company. This same scenario is unfolding across industries every day. In some cases, companies are exchanging market spaces. Many traditional airlines are now treating passengers as if they are their budget counterparts, whereas some low-cost airlines provide better services than many flag carriers.

Industries are increasingly being bypassed by ingenuity. Companies that insist on identifying with one area of business are the most vulnerable to extinction. Tomorrow is not so far off that it can be ignored. If you don't think about the future, you don't know where your competitors will come from, and you won't know where the opportunities lie.

THE PROMISE OF POSSIBILITY

Thinking about megatrends to analyze current events is a mental muscle. It must be exercised to become routine. Like any fitness program or fad, the benefits are only felt when the activity is practiced on a continual basis.

We've talked about fear of the unknown and its crippling effects. If you don't understand where you are right now or where you're headed, the path is uncertain, and it can be scary. If, however, you know where you are, and you have some idea of where you are going, the path is exciting. It's like when you're planning a trip to a new country or city. You don't know exactly what's in store, but you've mapped out how to get there, where to stay, and the things you'd like to see, do, and eat. Technically, the path ahead is "unknown," but you would never think of it that way, especially in relation to travel. You are more likely to think, *This is exciting! I can't wait to explore what's ahead of me.*

We tend to think of the future as unknown, because we don't know enough about what is happening around us. With a subtle shift in mindset, we might take a new approach toward the future. Instead of ignoring it or hoping it will just go away, we can examine the possibilities with an eye toward adventure.

What do we know right now? What are some of the things that could happen from this point forward? Although the future is not known, these questions can cause the future to be *less unknown*. Even if you don't know what is going to happen tomorrow, you are in control of the processes that are developed today, which removes some of the fear. In fact, we define the future as an empowering mechanism.

DRIVE is the ultimate framework to build and sustain the mental muscle necessary to evaluate current events and unearth opportunities for tomorrow. It is a relatively easy means of looking at the interconnectivity between the trends. Using the model, people can start interpreting and codifying reality to be more effective in their day-to-day lives. Because DRIVE is so applicable to the world around us, it triggers a stimulus inside the brain. It helps us take the first step toward thinking in terms of megatrends.

We use the framework in our own lives every day to better understand what is happening around us. Yes, questions will always remain, but DRIVE is a GPS system that gives you the lay of the land. It tells you there is water on the right and mountains on the left. There is a hairpin turn coming up soon, and you're approaching a town. It provides you with the key points of interest so you can stay focused on a course of action. Will you stop in the town or rest for a while by the water? What's of interest to you on the road ahead?

Many famous business frameworks can be boiled down into simple concepts, such as the well-known Five Forces or the SWOT analysis. In that respect, DRIVE is no different. By considering the five megatrends, we now have a simple tool and a starting point to make sense of our current reality that allows us to assess the future.

DRIVE IS DIFFERENT

We are the first to recognize that the discussion of megatrends is not new. Consulting firms and business analysts have been talking about demographics, resource scarcity, technological advances, and urbanization for decades with an eye toward predicting specific outcomes. In most cases, the research is presented as a Pandora's box with the message that the future is bleak—we should all head for the hills and take cover. Their purpose is to inform a fixed client base or pique the interest of potential clients. Because they are catering to a specific audience, the reports tend to provide a time-sensitive, generic overview with a heavy emphasis on business. They describe what is happening right now. The purpose and incentive behind that approach is selling their services. This is the reason why the social aspects of trends are hardly mentioned. The issue of inequalities is rarely featured in such research even though it is becoming clear that it is affecting how the future could unfold.

We are fortunate we don't have the same constraints. DRIVE is different, because it is far more encompassing, comprehensive, universal, and timeless. The framework is evergreen and applicable to all situations at all times. We envision this book to be a time-*insensitive* machine to connect trends and the relationship among those trends today and into the future. When someone picks up this book twenty years from now, DRIVE will still be a relevant tool to decipher world events. Naturally, at that time, events would be very different, but trends will remain a useful lens to understand our new surroundings.

Our approach is not sensationalistic, instructional, or predictive but placid and, in many instances, even cautious. The DRIVE framework allows you to think about all the implications an action could have: economic, social, personal, and global. Using DRIVE, our intention is to educate people and help them to think in a new way—a way that will be just as informative and enlightening tomorrow as it is today.

CHAPTER 2
WHAT IS THE DRIVE FRAMEWORK?

—

Our journey to DRIVE began with competitiveness—a concept that explores the challenges and constraints posed by global competition. Take currency devaluation as an example. Many people still hail this as an advantage to compete—witness how the drop in the value of the pound sterling is seen by many as good fortune. The UK can now export more and more cheaply even though it is also importing even more. Sure, devaluation allows countries to boost export. At the same time, they are effectively selling their own people on the cheap, which does not serve to enhance the standard of living.

We started to look at ways to improve competitiveness.

One of the problems is that it's a country-specific way of looking at the world. When you examine a country's macroeconomic data, you're looking at what is happening there *right now*. Although the data identifies potentially promising markets, those markets don't necessarily offer a lot of growth opportunities for individuals or businesses.

We were dissatisfied with the limited scope of the existing perspectives and wanted to identify what the underlying forces that drive future change actually are, not just country by country but worldwide. What characteristics or activities generate waves of change regardless of where you happen to be?

After digging into the existing frameworks and analysis, we came to the conclusion that any aggregate measure of growth was partial to a linear model, which is no longer applicable across the board in a global economy. "History is written by the winners" is an accurate phrase. Past and future casting gives you only part of the story, because you're not able to see the whole picture.

The truth is, different countries are achieving different things. Terence is specifically focused on the variances within the emerging economies of BRIC (Brazil, Russia, India, and China). Each country in that bloc performs so differently; they're almost incomparable from an achievement perspective.

Policy makers often want to see their countries playing a bigger role in the digital world. Some of them think getting young people into developing new apps is not only cool but also gives them a great career. If you look deeper, you realize that the app economy is already maturing. The twenty most successful app developers account for almost half of all the revenue on Apple's app store. At the same time, a quarter of all downloaded apps are uninstalled after a single use.[1]

Next, we started to look at things on a grassroots level and noticed several significant breakthroughs. We looked at everything from the renowned Silicon Valley start-ups that became multibillion-dollar companies all the way to Skype—based in Estonia, a small, lesser-known country—suddenly a player on the global field.

The story behind DRIVE started with the process of elimination. It wasn't about the principles of aggregation, or the specific behaviors within emerging economies, or the macrodata; it was about something else. As opposed to the traditional top-down approach, we started to recognize

---

1 http://www.economist.com/news/business-and-finance/21696477-market-apps-maturing-now-one-text-based-services-or-chatbots-looks-poised

an abundance of bottom-up opportunities. In fact, they were popping up everywhere.

For example, just because the United States might be the most advanced country in the world for certain technologies doesn't mean it is going to be the driving force behind all of the world's groundbreaking innovations in the future. It may not even be where the opportunities lie—not by a long shot. China, for instance, offers many lessons its Western counterparts should learn in terms of running successful Internet businesses.[2] You have an increased chance of harnessing opportunities when you look at them from a bottom-up approach.

PRESENT!

To get away from the "trap" of macrothinking, we started to look at what's happening now. How do we define growth today? Where are markets growing quickly? We don't know what's going to happen tomorrow, but we can tell you where it is raining or where the sun is shining right now. Our focus shifted away from the past and the future to a contemporary perspective.

Our vocabulary is restricted by forward-looking words,

---

2 http://www.economist.com/news/business/21703428-chinas-wechat-shows-way-social-medias-future-wechats-world

such as *forecasting* and *predicting* and backward-looking ones, such as *benchmarking*. We don't spend enough time looking at the present. If something is going to happen in the future, the seeds of that activity are taking root today. In the absence of an appropriate existing term, we refer to this practice as present-casting. The intention is to bring people's focus to what is happening now.

With DRIVE, we are able to look at the whole picture and the evolution of specific questions we face. We are not honoring the past to determine the future; we are honoring the present. In this way, DRIVE is not an intermediary between backcasting and forecasting; it is an entirely new and different approach. By understanding what is really happening today, we have a much better chance of finding the right capabilities and developing the right strengths to meet the challenges of the future. The goal is to make more informed choices now.

Looking into the future is easier than looking at today. Due to the worsening air pollution, electric cars have been hailed as a promising solution. By one estimate, London will have some 20,000 electric cars by 2020. And this would possibly grow by five times to 100,000 in the five years that follow.[3]

---

3   Transport for London, *An Ultra Low Emission Vehicle Delivery Plan for London: Cleaner Vehicles for a Cleaner City*, July 2015.

There is only one slight problem: the distribution network cannot support it. "London's 120-year-old power grid may not be able to support such large numbers of electric cars charging without significant reinforcement," Marc Coltelli, a director in the Global Power & Utilities practice at EY, a global business advisory company, told us.[4]

"The problem is not the generation of power. Instead, it is the capacity of the network," said Gareth Wynn, senior managing director of energy and natural resources at FTI Consulting, a global business advisory firm.[5]

From there, we ask traditional, cause-and-effect-type questions. What must we have in place to achieve *X*? We look at limited specificities in the absence of certain diffuse elements. We dissect what is happening now and select only the things we want to think about and plan for, or only those things that apply specifically to the electric car industry.

THE EVOLUTION OF DRIVE

We started to think in terms of cause and effect but on a much larger spectrum. Social change affects the chemistry of the planet from a human perspective or demographic,

---

4 Interview with Marc Coltelli, May 4, 2016.
5 Interview with Gareth Wynn, May 25, 2016.

but resources are also directly impacted. When there is an uneven distribution of resources across a population, inequalities occur. The evolution between the first three megatrends is easy for most people to understand.

The first engine of the framework was to build on our experiences and discussions with different people both inside and outside of the classroom. We looked for the one constant, which was social change, and then we built out the consequent tangents: resource scarcity and inequalities. At that point, all of the work we had done in the past started to come together. Our individual and collective research around sustainability, economy, finance, inequality, and unemployment converged like a river confluent in the same direction. We were simply building on our own understanding of the world. *D, R,* and *I* were the foundational blocks of the framework. They are all mainstream megatrends that governments and policy makers are already considering and designing for.

Volatility, scale, and complexity came into the mix with the realization that the mathematical model we'd been using for decades to measure risk or define value was no longer applicable. The model did not translate accurately from a rich country to a poor country, but the concept of volatility certainly did. Most people think about the stock market when they hear the word, but to us, volatility represents the unpredictability of various shifts and changes—to the markets, to our work environments, and to the global business landscape.

Volatility can be aptly used in discussions around robotics, blockchains, and artificial intelligence (AI), which are going to change the way the world works on a massive scale. These innovations will be like electricity or the Internet: they will change everything on the face of the earth. Most people don't understand the full implications.

Although we know they're going to be huge, we have no concrete way to predict how robotics, blockchains, and AI will impact businesses, job markets, and society overall. For this reason, we include complexity of scale in the conversations around volatility, because it's difficult to appreciate the scale of change before us, but it needs to be considered.

Then, *E*, or enterprising dynamics, came in response to the gigantic ocean of activity as another means of change. *E* is the element of the acronym that is updated on an almost-daily basis. The way a company innovates today is very different than the way it innovated yesterday. The story is always changing. We are seeing companies adapt faster to new technologies, offerings, and solutions. Because *V* and *E* are not immediately obvious discussion points regarding megatrends or the future, they allow for a richer and deeper conversation.

A little more than a year ago, we were at a conference in Singapore. Although we had been working on DRIVE for some time, this was our first time presenting it in public. Terence had sketched everything out in his leather bound journal: our frustration with the aggregate model of yesteryear, the limitations of macro- and microeconomics, and our work to create a framework for looking at today to better prepare for tomorrow. With that sketch of his perfectly represented DRIVE, it was like putting on a pair of magnifying glasses. Suddenly, the world appeared much clearer. A lively conversation ensued, and since that day, we've been testing and presenting DRIVE to different groups around the world.

A LOOK AT WHAT CAME BEFORE

As self-proclaimed rebels, we have a hard time teaching traditional economics classes. Neither of us can get behind many of the concepts with conviction. We both feel we can create more benefits for our students by talking about various economic activities that are happening in real time, all around us, than we can by lecturing them endlessly about a theory that was conceived when the world was a different place. We focus on current events and then explain the economic mechanisms behind them. The hope is that our students will learn about theory in the context of real life.

When we took this approach, a few questions arose time and again. The first was: "What is really happening in the eurozone?" The second was: "What is really happening with China, and how did it become so economically powerful?" The traditional business school curriculum does not put enough emphasis on bringing different subject matters together. They're still using a silo approach. Students have been unable to form a big-picture worldview.

We decided to develop a course that brought all of the different economic disciplines together. We wanted to help students understand what was happening in all directions. The course was called Business 360.

Simultaneously, we had been writing articles for the *Financial Times*[6],[7] and *Harvard Business Review*[8] about how and why business schools need to change. Our feeling was that business school professors should be more like movie directors, "orchestrating and coaching a multinational cast of actors through experiments, and stepping

---

6 https://www.ft.com/content/d86935bc-73ea-11e4-82a6-00144feabdc0
7 https://www.ft.com/content/d35a87de-1411-11e5-abda-00144feabdc0
8 https://hbr.org/2014/07/resumes-are-messing-up-hiring

off of the stage for a broader purview. This new frontier demands something inconceivable from professors: Risk not knowing what the outcome would be, or the metrics associated to it, *a priori*."[9]

When we took the Business 360 concept outside of the classroom, we further discovered that it wasn't just MBA students who were having a hard time connecting the dots. Executives and professionals in the real world also had a very silo approach to looking at the world. Most of them couldn't see beyond their own back door. With a specific set of objectives and activities, they were not able to effectively look at the big picture either.

Nevertheless, everyone—students, executives, professionals, and fellow academics—wanted to know where tomorrow's opportunities were. The question came at us from every imaginable direction. We did our best to provide thoughtful, comprehensive answers, but we're not fortune-tellers, and we don't call ourselves forecasters either. We're academics looking at the world around us and trying to make sense of it all.

In an attempt to identify new business and market opportunities, we focused on finding areas that were growing

---

[9] https://hbr.org/2014/05/business-school-professors-should-be-like-movie-directors

by at least 15 percent on an annual basis. We set up the parameters of what defined fast-emerging markets (FEMs) and enlisted the help of our students to find them. When given an assignment with this level of specificity, our researchers came back with solid support data. They discovered more than fifty pockets of excellence across the globe abiding to an exceptional rate of growth. They never aggregated or became strong enough to the degree that their impact changed the GDP of their country. These areas, we found, do not just exist in emerging economies such as China, India, and Brazil. They were found in Japan, Italy, and France as well.

From there, we came up with some proxies to better define FEMs. They were recurrent conditions such as weather events, government initiatives, or shocks that created a trajectory in that particular market.

For example, the legalization of marijuana is a recent government initiative in the Unites States. Some state laws were altered, and a new market opportunity cracked wide open. Although the market existed illegally for decades, government decriminalization and legalization of a single plant generated an immediate open market with a visible system to support it—pharmacies, doctors, patients, edibles, and other marijuana-related products.

There are other cases where policies have been in place for years without much activity, such as wind energy in Scotland. It wasn't until 2005 and 2006 that private investors started to build windmills in western Scotland. When they did, revenue was generated at record speeds, and renewable energy was suddenly available.

Although we identified structural parameters, we could not come up with a precise sequence of events. There didn't appear to be a clear A, B, C, and then D pathway toward new opportunity, but the structure conditions we identified at the outset were always present. FEMs were a well-received topic, because a lot of people are interested in learning how to define tomorrow's growth opportunities. We were invited to speak at conferences around the world, and we continued our research.

We noticed that explaining FEMs on their own was not enough to contextualize the string of events that led to specific business opportunities. However, when the framework of DRIVE is applied to the examination of FEMs, suddenly those opportunities make sense. The megatrends are the lens from which to understand FEMs; they are the pathways to the destination everyone is trying to locate. All of our research and work was coming full circle.

HOW TO USE DRIVE

DRIVE is a foundation to help people start making sense of reality and the future. It illuminates the blind spots that cause so many people to run and hide in fear. However, it is not a prescriptive formula. DRIVE is a reflective instrument. It's like an insight generator because it provides us a way to engage in difficult questions. It tells us that we need to think about today in a critical manner. So how do we do this?

Each of the five components of DRIVE has a relationship to the others. Not one of them exists independently. We've found it sufficiently clear, when presenting the framework, that everyone on a global level can agree *D, R, I, V,* and *E* exist everywhere in the world.

DRIVE is a starting point. The five elements don't guarantee that we will reach our destination, but they will guide us on our journey to get there. Every person and organization that utilizes the framework will define their own understanding of how to use it. Their engagement with the framework will be in the context of the specific questions they are trying to address. In that regard, DRIVE is like a springboard that can be used in a variety of contexts to ask a host of compelling questions. There is tremendous flexibility in how and where it can be used and for what purpose, because it connects the dots on a mega level.

One of the main challenges we've heard regarding DRIVE, especially as it relates to FEMs, is, where's the data to back this up? People always look for, in particular, quantitative data as validation to support a premise. The interpretation of data is based on the value of judgment, and that value is the qualitative interpretation of the number. If you are looking for data, we can assume you know what the answer could be, or you are looking for a certain answer. In either case, you are already placing restrictions on the possible outcome and being blinded to what could happen. Plus, there have been several occasions where something makes sense mathematically, but it does not make sense realistically.

We want to make it very clear, right up front, that DRIVE is *intentionally not data driven*. It's about understanding a concept, and therefore, DRIVE doesn't have a formula, an algorithm, or an equation that dictates the findings. On the contrary, our intention is to get people to open their minds, to be open to possibilities, and to look at the current circumstances with a fresh set of eyes. We do not want people to walk away from the framework and form a hypothesis that needs to be backed up by data.

We envision someone might engage with DRIVE because he or she is curious about resource scarcity in his or her environment. He or she could use the framework and never even think about D, R, I, V, or E. It's entirely that person's prerogative. We don't dictate how to use it. There is no right or wrong way.

Our hope is that people will ask open-minded questions and take a qualitative research approach to the framework. We care about the process and the details the process uncovers. We care about the interconnectedness of world events and activities and how one thing affects another. It's not about evaluating the correlation between two contrasting sets of data. It's about taking things into consideration that you may not have thought about before.

When you start to open up and think about the different possibilities of the future, your awareness is elevated. It's similar to scenario planning, a method that Mark teaches, which gets the brain juices flowing. It causes you to be more alert and sensitive to what is really happening in a business landscape from all perspectives. By looking at economic, political, and social changes all together, you get a deeper understanding of an event or activity.

Scenario planning is used to make long-term plans, whereas strategic planning implies the identification of all the steps necessary to achieve those plans. For example, if you were planning to run a marathon, your training regime would vary slightly every day in intensity until you have built up the endurance to complete the race. You are taking a strategic approach to achieve the desired outcome: How will I complete a marathon? If, on the other hand, you wanted to look at something such as how the energy revolution will impact the price of gas, you would take a scenario approach when examining the question. Scenario planning works well with questions where you cannot directly control the outcome.

DRIVE has become the precursor for Mark's instruction for scenario planning. He asks clients or students to first analyze their own industry or question within the context of the megatrends. Setting the stage in this manner leads to higher quality, more thoughtful discussions. DRIVE essentially becomes a tool that helps to simplify the complexity of what's happening in the world today and in the future. It helps people move from being immobile and paralyzed to actually owning the conversation. Therefore, not only is it reflective and all-encompassing, it is also empowering. Better questions lead to more informed responses.

By using DRIVE, the concept of "the future" becomes more of a fluid thought process. We know we cannot control it or understand it, but because we are considering the many possibilities, it becomes less disarming. The future doesn't unfold because we added one plus one. It unfolds because it's inevitable; a number of variables generate an outcome. We understand it is something that will happen over time. It's a process of evolution. Whatever we decide today could impact the future, but it doesn't dictate the future. DRIVE serves to reframe the conversation so people have more confidence to face whatever is "out there" on the horizon.

PART 2

THE REALITY OF TODAY

CHAPTER 3

D: DEMOGRAPHIC AND SOCIAL CHANGES

At the first mention of megatrends, we are consistently challenged about the future and what it looks like. After reminding people we are not crystal ball readers, the conversation begins with *D*, which represents demographic and social changes. People are a natural starting point; they are the atoms of our planet and the center of any discussion about a future state.

POPULATION

When looking at tomorrow, why do demographics matter? Historically, the population pyramid told us where we were headed. A friend of ours, Roland Schatz, CEO of

Media Tenor International AG, mentioned over lunch a while ago that if you looked at the population pyramid for Germany, you would know what would happen in the future with near-absolute certainty. The first observation is that in ten to fifteen years' time, Germany will be in the grips of a pension crisis. Increasing numbers of people will age, but they will be supported by a decreasing number of young people.

Just as interesting as that is today, the largest segment of the population are those aged forty to fifty-five. The majority of them are taxpayers at the height of their earning power, which means that Germany is currently collecting the most taxes from the largest group of people in the country. They're enjoying a financial heyday, to say the least.

At the same time, Germany is operating on a deficit budget and has not invested enough in its own infrastructure. This tells us that not only will they face a pension crisis in the next ten to fifteen years as their largest population ages, but also their ability to collect tax revenue from that same group will deteriorate.[1] These two factors alone put Germany and a good number of other developing countries in economic and social peril. Addressing these threats is

---

1   http://blogs.lse.ac.uk/eurocrisispress/2015/03/12/germany-the-giant-with-the-feet-of-clay/

imperative. This story, although exemplifying and contextual to a specific country, is why we begin our discussion of megatrends with demographic and social changes.

As we learned more about the issue, we discovered a multitude and a latitude of subsequent topics within demographics. A country's GDP is directly related to population growth, as are fertility rates, life expectancies, health care, urbanization, and certainly, access to resources. The distribution of resources is directly related to how many people are living in a given area. Our ability to pay for pensions is directly related to how many children we have and how long we live.

Suddenly, *D* became a huge topic. When we teach it, the discussion lasts for hours. It is the anchor for understanding the interconnectivity of world events. Demographic and social changes impact the way that companies operate because aging affects consumption. Consumption impacts how products are manufactured, which also affects revenue. When the population ages, architecture, design, and building changes to accommodate people with disabilities. The ripple effect is in full swing.

Demographics, no matter where you look, affect everything. It is the most important part of DRIVE because it sets the tone for the discussion and triggers the proper mindset. In some ways, *D* is like a Trojan horse; one conversation can easily lead to fifteen others, and they are all equally relevant to everyone. No one is immune.

As discussed earlier, the population pyramid was one of the best predictors of the future of an economy. In the past, children made up the largest section of the pyramid, dominating its foundational base. As people aged, the pyramid narrowed toward its peak, but for all of history, the shape was always a pyramid, indicating children zero to four and five to nine, as the largest segments of our society.

In the last four decades, though, the number of kids people are having is decreasing in several places throughout the world. Better education, nutrition, and access to health care contribute to the trend. Wealthier countries have more family planning services available, and the role and structures of the family have changed. Children are no longer the largest part of the population, and there are an equal number of people in the segment aged zero to forty-nine.

Today, the bottom of many pyramids is narrowing while the pyramids themselves are getting taller, so much so that we should start calling it the age "shard," referring to the iconic building of London. In fact, we could be seeing more shards getting taller.

The impact this transformation will have on society is profound, although often underrepresented by the media. With an increase of close to 300 percent of the older age group, those aged eighty-five and older, the pyramid will transform itself even more with a segment of our population that will become more prominent than now. This changes health care, consumption, products, and eventually, markets. It is a perfect example of the type of information we can glean about a certain future by observing the trends right now.

Population trends are country specific. Not everyone is headed in the same direction, which adds another level of complexity to the matter. Projections show that most populations of developed countries will be over forty years old by 2030, and fifty-two in Japan. While China has a younger population (37.0) today than the United States (38.0), by 2030, it will be 43.2 compared to 40.0—China's aging population is "catching up" with the developed world.[2]

Except for Japan, South Korea, and Cuba, all aging countries are in Europe and are the result of the combination of very high life expectancy and very low fertility rates.

---

2   https://www.rolandberger.com/publications/publication_pdf/roland_berger_trend_compendium_2030___trend_1_demographic_dynamics.pdf

This creates challenges for social security systems and financing pensions.

Meanwhile, the most youthful are the developing countries of the sub-Saharan region and are the result of very low levels of life expectancy and very high levels of fertility. This creates challenges for educating the population and providing them with employment. The world's population will plateau for the first time in human history, creating an insufficient labor force to support the old-age pensioners. With the labor pool shrinking, the only way to increase economic growth is through continuous investments. The past shows that productivity significantly increases in industries that are not protected, which means that governments need to introduce more liberal competitive prices.

One reason for the narrowing bottom of the pyramid is the drop in fertility. Declining fertility rates don't just impact the sheer number of people on the planet. The entire dynamic of the family unit changes, too. The family is a quintessential part of civilization. The world's societies are based on a succession model between parents and their kids. The number of kids has traditionally determined the degree of inherited wealth from one generation to another. How does that change impact nuclear families and how they relate to each other?

For example, Mark is an only child, but his father had five siblings and his mother had eight. Consider the dissonance between Mark's experiences of family versus his parents'. Mark's grandparents had a certain expectation of how society would be, but the way society behaves is different. Society wasn't designed to accommodate childless couples or women who don't have kids, and yet today, almost 50 percent of women in the United States are childless.[3]

The fact that more and more women are choosing not to have children brings up some ethical questions. It could be argued that they are not contributing to the certainty of future generations, but they are reaping the benefits of the generations who have paved the way for them to enjoy their current freedom of choice. Do humans have the responsibility to ensure the viability of future generations, and if so, how does that responsibility mesh with the principles of sustainable development and protecting the world's diminishing resources? If the trend toward having fewer children continues, as it's projected to do, who will support our kids when they get old? There are so many different conversations that spring up from the fertility rate question. A big one is: "What will society look like when the entire structure of it has been changed?"

---

3 http://www.huffingtonpost.com/2015/04/09/childless-more-women-are-not-having-kids-says-census_n_7032258.html

URBANIZATION

Urbanization is the result of a lot more than a shift in the population pyramid. People tend to go where the jobs are. In decades past, when society was more heavily centered on agriculture, jobs were found on farms in the country. People were spread out and lived and worked across the land. Towns with a higher population concentration offered access to services and products that were not accessible in the country. Eventually, some of those towns grew into cities, depending on resource availability and infrastructure.

Even though today many people work remotely, there is still a human desire to work together, so more and more people have migrated toward the cities. Even if they're not working with one another directly, they still want to be in the same space. This is evident in the pop-up workspaces and entrepreneurial incubators sprouting up all over major cities. As social animals, humans are naturally drawn toward being together.

Urbanization is happening with increasing frequency all over the world. Governments encourage it because it is easier and cheaper to provide the necessary infrastructure when people live in clustered groups. Urbanization brings increased revenue on a local level, which circles back to building a better infrastructure. Indeed, greater urbanization appears to have a positive effect on GDP development, and countries with the highest urbanization ratios are showing the greatest GDP per head of the population.[4] This is partially the reason why China's urbanization ratio rose from 21 percent to 56 percent in the thirty years between 1982 and 2015. It seeks to push it to 60 percent by 2020, giving its cities more importance in economic development.[5]

Cities, as a result, get more and more powerful economically, if not also politically. Larger cities attract more people and talent, as well as both domestic and foreign investments, which, in turn, can create more jobs that attract more talent. This expanding talent pool can affect corporate decisions; the world-renowned foldable-bicycle manufacturer Brompton decided to remain in London to expand the manufacturing capacity.[6]

There are pros and cons to urbanization. On the downside, there are obvious space and capacity constraints with overcrowding. From an individual perspective, it is easier to find work in a city, simply because of the economy of scale. More people equals more opportunities. However,

[4] "China's Urban Dreams and the Regional Reality," *Economist Intelligence Unit* (2014).

[5] https://www.bloomberg.com/view/articles/2016-07-19/has-china-reached-peak-urbanization

[6] http://www.telegraph.co.uk/finance/newsbysector/industry/engineering/11807765/Brompton-Bicycle-to-move-to-bigger-London-factory.html

the cost to live in the city is significantly higher, and you get less space for the money. It's a toss-up.

Simultaneously, as more and more businesses gravitate toward online sales, business location is less important than it once was. Depending on what type of business you have, it doesn't matter if your customers live in a village or in a booming metropolis, as long as they have immediate access to your product or service. It also means you don't necessarily need to headquarter your business in an expensive city and pay exorbitant rent.

Because people tend to go where the jobs are, they're moving away from what we have in abundance—land. The housing stock hasn't increased substantially enough to accommodate urbanization, particularly in megacities, so where does housing come from? The housing that exists becomes more expensive or people live outside of the city centers where housing is more affordable. In Europe, most of the young people starting out in their careers have no choice but to co-rent with a roommate or two. Starting salaries are low, and they probably have student debts to pay off.

Trying to raise a family in a big city is also cost prohibitive. This is where urbanization and the declining fertility rate overlap. When having kids means living in a shoebox to try to make ends meet, many urban professionals will decide to put having a family on the back burner. This is particularly true in the megacities, which are defined as cities with more than ten million people.

Increasing urbanization also changes how things "flow" through the cities. As cities and towns become ever-more urbanized, it may become harder to predict the possible outcomes. Matt Hotson, the UK CFO of RSA, a global insurance company, said, "Runoff water after rainfall no longer follows a specific pattern, given how the number of properties and cars are cramping together and the layout is becoming more dynamic."[7]

Getting people to be able to flow has also become challenging as more and more people are living together. For instance, Kevin Craven, CEO of Central Government Services at SERCO, one of the largest international professional service providers in the world, told us recently, "Worsening traffic has made the sixteen thousand movements a month of ferrying people between courts and prisons more and more difficult."[8]

"Continuous investments in upgrading the infrastructure are therefore key to keeping cities going. With urbanization

---

[7] Interview with Matt Hotson, June 20, 2016.
[8] Interview with Kevin Craven, November 18, 2016.

comes the need to invest in infrastructures including transport, clean water supply, wastewater management, and power supply. There is also a need to think about the general environmental issues. For instance, with global warming comes more flooding. This will mean investing in flood barriers," said Mel Zuydam, European CFO of ch2M, a global engineering, consulting, design, program management, construction, and operations company.

He adds, "Urbanization and population growth in London has meant the Victorian-age sewer system is at overcapacity; as a result, we are engaged in delivering a new state-of-the-art 'supersewer' to serve the city, a giant tunnel running under the River Thames, fully privately funded, which will transform the health and environment of the River Thames."[9]

Even though the cost to upgrade an infrastructure is astronomical, it is a must if cities want to continue to grow and stay competitive. Take Toronto, for instance. After thirty years since it was first tabled, the city finally has a rapid railway connecting downtown and the airport in 2015. It was one of the world's leading business and financial centers that did not have a dedicated airport express.[10]

---

9 Interview with Mel Zuydam, July 15, 2016.
10 http://www.metrolinx.com/en/docs/pdf/board_agenda/20160223/20160223_ BoardMtg_UP_Express_Presentation_EN.pdf

When looking at urbanization, it is important to understand the ways that cities grow and how they become powerful economic destinations. We expect the geostrategic equilibrium to change in the next ten, fifteen, or twenty years, and new cities will rise in prominence while others diminish in popularity.

Look at a city like Detroit. Not all that long ago, it was the auto industrial capital of the United States. Due to a variety of industry-specific economic and political factors, Detroit is a shadow of its former self. It doesn't take much for cities to topple: political instability, social unrest, or a natural disaster can take a town down and cause it to be less relevant on the global scale.

We could argue that the uprise of new automotive clusters or conglomerates in the world—in Hungary, Slovakia, Poland, and China, to name a few of the newly emerged automotive hubs—have reduced significantly the importance of Detroit as a city. Our argument about urbanization and social changes is that they not only change population flows, but they also transform economic realities and change the map of where our most significant economic geographies are located. We can expect this trend to continue in the next decades, as new cities will emerge as new power hubs.

THE REAL EFFECTS OF AGING

The algorithm for calculating what everything in society should look like is no longer valid. The entire process of preparing for the future was built on the population pyramid, which as discussed, is reversing. Trying to use old numbers to fit the new reality adds stress on top of change—an unfortunate combination.

Consider unemployment subsidies. To manage a common rate of unemployment, the government calculates that a certain percentage of the population will be out of work for eight to twelve months. Some of those people will find jobs much sooner, and others may take up to fifteen months or more. The calculation evens out if reality matches up to the projected statistics, which it rarely does. That calculation is usually done by assuming that population trends won't alter too much from one data point in time to another. However, the algorithm falls apart if people are without jobs for more than eighteen months because the changes in our social structure make us less productive, and therefore, it takes longer for people to find employment. We saw this happen not too long ago in the United States after the financial collapse. Unemployment subsidies no longer made sense. We are facing a similar threat when it comes to health-care costs combined with longer life expectancies.

LIFE EXPECTANCY AND AGING

The global trend toward longer life expectancy is an immediate concern. But how much does it cost to live longer? Just because people are living longer does not mean they are living healthier or the quality of living is better. What impact does an aging, unhealthy population have on the health-care system? The situation could be catastrophic as costs mount, and the cities fill to capacity with elderly sick people.

Economics dictate that any economy can only expand its output either by raising the amount of labor or raising the productivity of individual labor. As the general population is getting older, the only way for economies to continue to increase their output is by productivity gains. Yet, labor force aging could reduce such gains. While experience makes older workers more productive than the others, they may find it difficult to take up new technologies, which could have an adverse effect on innovations.[11]

As the older workers tend to get paid more, they are taking more of the wealth but also curbing innovation. The opposite is true for the younger generation. They can become more productive but are not as well or proportionally compensated. These older people are richer than

---

11 Sylvain Broyer, Thibault Cuillère, and Stéphane Houri, *Silver Economy: An Opportunity for France* (Paris: Natixis Research, October 10, 2016).

the young and have more spending power. For instance, in 1981, a French thirty-three-year-old had the highest purchasing power of all age brackets. Now, forty-six-year-olds hold the title.[12] Interesting, then, that most of the new consumer products are geared toward the younger crowds. The so-called silver market or silver economy (*le papy-boom* in French) is still somehow off the radar of many companies.

Aging is not only relevant to consumer or health-care markets. It also matters in other less visible places. Take prisons, for example. Kevin Craven, a CEO at SERCO (mentioned previously), told us that the average age of the inmates is now growing rapidly. Last year, for instance, the number of prisoners over the age of sixty grew by more than 9 percent. As a result, "prisons now need to think about residential care, nursing, dementia issues, lifts versus stairs [note: lifts/elevators are confined spaces that prisons want to avoid], as well as the design of prisons—do they need to be as secure for elderly prisoners?"[13]

HEALTH CARE

While it may sound like good news that people are living longer, it's only half of the story. The economic

---

12   Ibid.
13   Interview with Kevin Craven, November 18, 2016.

repercussions of living longer have the potential to be devastating. As we age, productivity diminishes as our bodies start to fail. Unhealthy people become a financial burden on the rest of society. The rise of health epidemics such as diabetes, obesity, cancer, and other diseases could have a potential domino effect on public spending and debt. We keep people alive longer, but the quality of their lives decreases, and our social infrastructure carries the costs.

One of our friends is a medical doctor at Massachusetts General Hospital in Boston. She told us, "Obamacare covers only twenty cents on the dollar for medical costs. Hospitals and doctors cannot refuse service to anyone, but they are not incentivized to provide immediate and prompt care. In fact, they're punished for it. When people call to make appointments, they are not turned away, but they cannot get in to see the doctor for several weeks. The medical establishment is operating on an increased delay as its own costs climb and there are more sick people to deal with."

Similar problems are happening in the UK. It has been reported that up to four patients a week are losing their eyesight because hospitals cannot keep up with demand for "follow-up" appointments. Even though hospitals are fined if patients wait more than eighteen weeks for a consultation or treatment after a general practitioner (GP) referral, there are no targets for follow-ups. In fact, the lack of data makes it difficult to determine the magnitude of the problem.[14]

China is woefully ill prepared for dementia. About nine million people in that country already have some form of dementia. In absolute terms, China has more than twice as many dementia sufferers than the United States. Some two-thirds of China's sufferers have Alzheimer's, which has tripled since 1990. The number of Alzheimer's patients may increase another fourfold between now and 2050.[15]

One of the greatest leap-forwards in the past few decades is that many people have risen above poverty, particularly in emerging economies. Although these people are living richer lives, they are not necessarily living better or higher quality lives. They still eat the same cheap, high-processed foods as they did before, only now they eat considerably more of it. The cheaper and more processed the food source becomes, the fewer nutrients and disease-fighting vitamins are present. Even though people are wealthier and living longer, childhood obesity is on the rise in

---

14 http://www.telegraph.co.uk/news/health/news/12196470/Hundreds-losing-sight-every-year-due-to-delays-in-NHS-follow-ups.html

15 http://www.economist.com/news/china/21693241-china-ill-prepared-consequence-ageing-lots-people-dementia-state-minds

China. A recent study revealed that twenty-nine years ago, there was hardly one obese child out of a hundred. That situation has drastically changed. In 2014, about one in six boys and one in eleven girls were obese.[16] Most people smoke cigarettes there as well, so China is facing—and will continue to face—an increase in cardiovascular disease, diabetes, and other complications as a result of the population being overweight and unhealthy. While many in India are now living above the poverty line, air pollution is so bad that half of Delhi's schoolchildren have permanently impaired lung capacity.[17]

A few years ago, Mark and his students researched the health-care costs during the last three months in the life of an American versus citizens of other countries. They found that the last three months of an American's health-care costs are equal to twelve years of health-care costs for a German. The reason comes down to accountability. US citizens tend to believe that if something happens to them, the doctor will fix them. It's a cultural expectation, which causes people to smoke cigarettes, ingest a variety of unhealthy foods, drive their motorcycles without helmets, opt out of health insurance, and take all manner

---

16 Ying-Xiu Zhang et al., "Trends in Overweight and Obesity among Rural Children and Adolescents from 1985 to 2014 in Shandong, China," *European Journal of Preventive Cardiology* 23, no. 12 (2016): 1314–20.

17 https://www.theguardian.com/commentisfree/2016/nov/08/the-guardian-view-on-air-pollution-ministers-must-act

of risk. Alternatively, European citizens tend to accept more responsibility for their own decisions. They don't shift the entire obligation to the doctor.

Doctors are tasked with being in the horrible position to tell family members and friends when someone has died, only to be met with shock and, more often than not, anger. Many Americans do not accept death as a natural process of life and view it almost as they would an accident or something that could be avoided. They want someone to pay for it, which only increases the cost of health care. The doctors get stuck in a vicious cycle. In an attempt to avoid legal trouble, they keep patients alive long after they should pass on, and the patient's quality of life suffers in turn.

To cover themselves financially, especially in the face of legal action, hospitals and doctors are forced to make decisions that put their patients at risk. For example, consider gastrointestinal bypass, a procedure conducted on people who are morbidly obese. The small intestine is reduced to two inches, and then the tissue is reconnected to the stomach. It is a highly risky operation and technically difficult to execute. To recoup costs, hospitals send people home after just a few days. Even though the operation itself is dangerous, the highest frequency of death occurs due to complications two to three days after surgery.

Inflated costs have a direct impact on the quality of medical service and the quality of patients' lives. Instead of health care being a means of serving other people, it has become a premium commodity, which increases administration costs. Our doctor friend told us that 40 percent of his hospital's budget goes to managing thirty-two different health insurance companies. That's a hard cost that is not going toward healing; it's allocated for administration fees alone.

In the last fifty years, the medical community has become more of a money grab than a public service. Hospitals cannot refuse service to people in need, but they don't know where the payment for their services will come from. Who is responsible: the individual, the insurance company, or the hospital? It's a financial game among the three parties that no one seems to be winning. Critical services, such as emergency care or long-term care, have been disrupted by demographic changes, and health has become a product.

Interestingly, we are also starting to see a shift toward more compassionate health care. Insurance companies are beginning to understand the importance of patient benefits over the bottom line. For example, in the United States, the prohibitive "preexisting" condition has been eliminated from the health-care paradigm. In the past, if a woman was pregnant and trying to obtain insurance, she would be denied coverage. Slowly, services are becoming more targeted to what people actually need and are therefore more humanized.

We can take a more evolved approach to life circumstances, based on individual health data, and pivot accordingly. Technology plays a large role in the collection of information through inventions such as the Fitbit. Wearable activity trackers allow individuals to take greater responsibility for their own health and longevity, instead of expecting health-care professionals to "fix" them. Those who want to live healthier, longer lives have access to the information that will allow them to do so. Together with the high cost and low efficiency and productivity in health-care industries, this has in part transformed these sectors from one that is based on sick care to well care and from one on patient to consumer.

On the other hand, insurance companies want to harness the customized, granular data as well. Traditional estimation techniques relied heavily on general demographic data based on averages. However, in order to offer policies appropriate for today's consumers, they need to look more closely at individualized information. Technology offers a better way to collect actuarial data.

Of course, there are still millions of people who could care less about their health. Either they cannot afford the technology to track their behaviors or the costs associated with living a healthier lifestyle, or they just can't be bothered. A pervasive and collective sense of entitlement exists in many nations throughout the world. For all of the increased awareness about health issues and access to personal information, disease and illness continue to be a reality.

RETIREMENT AGE

Because people are living longer, they're also working longer. The state pension they've paid into all of their lives is not enough to support them for twenty or more years of not working. For most people, there is no choice but to continue in their jobs—if they are able—long past the typical retirement age of sixty-five. They might be mentally ready to pull the trigger and retire, but they are not financially astute enough.

How will prolonged income earnings affect things such as asset management and insurance planning? Traditionally, when people retire, they turn to safer financial investments that can provide them with a fixed amount of income to ensure economic survival. But what happens when you (1) live much longer, so much so that you don't know how long your investment horizon beyond retirement would be, and (2) don't know if you should/could retire in order to be able to sustain yourself afterward?

Thus, the wealth management and pension sectors are gradually coming up with new products to meet emerging needs. Companies are offering more choices to help people manage their personal finances. Traditionally, older people held fewer growth products—that is, equity—in favor of stable cash and fixed-income investments. Now, as people are living longer and will most likely work longer, they are going to want—in fact, need—to have more and different products that allow them to grow their portfolios at an older age while also offering some protection. These nuances will have a huge impact on the wealth and asset management sectors.

TRANSFORMATION IS POSSIBLE

How can we effect positive societal change on a global level, and whose responsibility is it to lead the initiative? We can no longer rely on our governments to lead the charge. Politicians have lost our trust. People do not have confidence in what the government can or cannot do to effect real change. So, where are the influencers, and who are the decision makers of tomorrow, if not today?

Increasingly, change is coming from the bottom up. Individuals have more power than ever before, especially with the global soapbox that social media affords. To truly transform society, we need to find the leverage point that gives us quick access to a large number of people who are sharing constructive content. In the past, it took longer to evangelize people. Radio and TV messaging allowed for only one-directional exchanges. Today, 70 percent of the human race can be accessed through technology.

Social media and cell phone usage focuses on immediate engagement, interaction, and communication. The whole world's a stage, and we have the ability to interact with a global audience. Instead of using that access to manipulate or monetize one's own agenda, in the right hands, technology can be used to inform, improve, and empower people.

We have the technology, and we have the intention. Now we just need to execute by helping those two elements interface. Great ideas regarding humanitarian causes, entrepreneurship, and innovation exist all around us, but they don't scale to the level necessary to achieve truly great results. We can, however, achieve the desired results by tying the information and access we have at our fingertips to the DRIVE framework. Change is possible, and we advocate for it here, in the classroom, on the web, and everywhere that people are listening.

As demographics evolve, social infrastructure can adjust alongside it. We have the opportunity to reframe the narrative by updating our antiquated standards that were based on the old population pyramid. Although there is plenty of bad news out there, and some of what we talk about in DRIVE may sound dire, our true position is one of optimism and hope. Rather than expecting things to happen as a consequence of time going by, now is the right time for us—as business owners, policy makers, and individual citizens—to be empowered to make changes. Are you ready to embrace that degree of responsibility to change our future?

CHAPTER 4

R: RESOURCE SCARCITY

—

The scarcity of resources is certainly an issue when we look at it from a local perspective or in the context of a region or a country. However, the scarcity becomes less of a threat when we look at resources from a global, or planetary, perspective. If we could build more infrastructures to transport food and water resources to the areas that have less, we have the potential to enrich entire social and economic systems through increased manufacturing, energy sharing, and agriculture. Harmonizing on a global level reduces waste and helps to solve issues related to overproduction or poorly allocated resources.

When we talk about resource scarcity, the first thing that usually pops into people's minds is energy. When they think about energy, they think about oil. Many of our peers are not so old that they don't recall the oil shortage in 1973 when the United States reduced its domestic oil production and began to rely more heavily on imports from the Middle East. Costs went up, the politicians cried, "Crisis," and everyone went into a state of panic. Today, however, oil production in the United States is at an all-time high.[1] Energy, as a resource, is not a problem whatsoever. Indeed, many oil and gas sources are yet to be inventoried. Even if we do face an oil shortage in the future, we can still harness energy through wind and solar power.

Energy sources have made some rather interesting headlines. For example, between May 7 and 10, 2016, Portugal was running on only renewable—wind, solar, and hydro-generated energy for 107 consecutive hours, or more than four days.[2] On May 15, Germany was providing nearly all its electricity needs using clean energy only.[3]

Many Nordic countries are already claiming close to zero in their energy consumption; if not now, they will soon become a carbon-free economy. And they are set to have a greater variety of energy sources. Marc Barone, a managing director at AECOM, the global infrastructure services

---

1 http://www.huffingtonpost.com/roxana-maddahi/the-oil-crisis-in-plain-e_b_9268662.html
2 https://www.theguardian.com/environment/2016/may/18/portugal-runs-for-four-days-straight-on-renewable-energy-alone
3 http://www.independent.co.uk/environment/germany-just-got-almost-all-of-its-power-from-renewable-energy-a7037851.html

firm, told us, "As an alternative to using wind turbines, it might be possible to harness energy from sculptures and perhaps even statues when the wind rocks them."[4] An outlandish idea? Maybe. But this is what the Land Art Generator Initiative in Scotland set out to do. At the moment, the idea is still in its infancy, but it is robust enough to be tested and further developed.

The two global resources that are in immediate danger of scarcity are food and water. Not only is access to these resources in jeopardy, but the way they connect to some of the trends we discussed in *D*—demographic and social changes—also compounds the threat.

As more and more people move to the cities and urbanization increases, so too does the rate of consumption. The increased affordability grooms a booming "dining out" part of the service economy and several culinary options become available everywhere. From more upscale restaurants to varied cuisines, food has always been an indicator of economic activity across regions. People go out to eat more frequently, and food resources are stressed because the demand is higher. Cycles of consumption have become more sophisticated than ever before and transform the use of resources.

---

4   Interview with Marc Barone, November 29, 2016.

Naturally, demographic changes impact the availability of agricultural resources. Global consumption demands access to certain types of food year round. People expect to eat watermelon in winter and Swiss chard in summer. Products are shipped around the world to meet that demand. Agricultural methods have been altered with chemicals and fertilizers to produce more. The more chemicals that are used on plants, the wider the differentiation between species and hybrid species becomes.

At the top of this transformation, the biggest impact is visible on water consumption. Water is indeed at the center of resource scarcity. We use it for everything: agriculture, industrial production, and domestic needs. The output is outpacing the input.

The cycles of natural accessibility to resources are outnumbered by the cycles of consumption in the emerging economy. We are running out of resources, not because the planet does not produce enough, but because we are using them faster than they can be replenished. It is necessary to find better and faster ways of restoring what is used to eradicate the dangerous imbalance.

IMPLICATIONS OF RESOURCE SCARCITY

The implications of being able to feed are real and varied.

The increased consumption of meat has put other food under greater pressure. It takes two kilos of grain to create just one kilo of chicken; it takes about four to six kilos of grain for one kilo of lamb. For one kilo of beef, it can take anything from five to twenty kilos of grain.[5]

Food security comes into the sphere of politics. For example, the Chinese outsourced a good portion of their food production to the Russian Far East, a terribly underdeveloped section of the country, to secure their own supply. They rented land for planting, established farms, and hired local farmers to grow food. Economically speaking, it's a win-win economic relationship because the Chinese get their food supply and the Russians have employment.[6]

As for us consumers, one way to produce an ever-increasing amount of food is to systematically industrialize the process. And industry practices have sometimes reached the point of ethically questionable. Take the production of milk as an example. To continue a supply of animal milk, a farmer must have calves, kids, and lambs for suckling, but they also must be prevented from monopolizing the milk. One common method was to simply slaughter the

---

5   http://www.economist.com/blogs/feastandfamine/2013/12/livestock
6   Ben Judah, *Fragile Empire: How Russia Fell In and Out of Love with Vladimir Putin* (New Haven, CT: Yale University Press, 2013) contains a fascinating account of the relationship between China and the Russian Far East.

calves and kids shortly after birth, milk the mother, and then get her pregnant again.

A milk cow in this setting usually had a life span of five years before slaughter. Yet cows have a natural life span of about twenty years and can produce milk for eight or nine years.[7] Milk production years were reduced to five or less because of the stress caused by the conditions on factory farms that lead to disease, lameness, and reproductive problems.[8] During those five years, the cow was constantly pregnant. She was fertilized within 60 to 120 days after giving birth in order to preserve maximum milk production. The calves, on the other hand, were taken away shortly after birth. The females were reared to become milk cows and the males were slaughtered for meat.

If this makes poignant reading, a calf's life in a modern industrial meat farm is just as sad. In his book, *Sapiens*, historian Yuval Harari wrote:

> Immediately after birth the calf is separated from its mother and locked inside a tiny cage not much bigger than the calf's own body. There, the calf spends its

---

7   http://www.peta.org/issues/animals-used-for-food/animals-used-food-factsheets/cows-milk-cruel-unhealthy-product/

8   Ibid.

entire life—about four months on average. It never leaves its cage ... or even walks—all so that its muscles will not grow strong. Soft muscles mean a soft and juicy steak. The first time the calf has a chance to walk, stretch its muscles, and touch other calves is on its way to the slaughterhouse. In evolutionary terms, cattle represent one of the most successful animal species ever to exist. At the same time, they are some of the most miserable animals on the planet.[9,10]

There is a strong economic benefit for companies to become less dependent on water. A few are looking for smart ways to use less water and spend less money as a result. Some businesses have begun practicing better water efficiency through innovative technology. McDonald's in Europe is a great example. It partnered with a company called Urimat, which produces urinals for men's restrooms, among other things. The company discovered it is possible to produce entirely water-free urinals by replacing the water with sterilizing chemicals. McDonald's and Urimat have revolutionized water expenditure in European men's restrooms. With thousands of restaurants across the EU, not only was the switch to chemicals

---

9 Yuval Noah Harari, *Sapiens: A Brief History of Humankind* (New York: Vintage Book, 2011), 108.

10 Having read the above, Terence has from that moment cut down his meat consumption substantially. (Mark is already a vegetarian.) The information is that disturbing to him.

a great public relations move, but they are saving money while also protecting a limited natural resource and the environment.

If more companies understood that water efficiency equals good business, there is potential for the idea to scale. We like to imagine a world in which mom-and-pop businesses and smaller companies can emulate the practices of larger companies and reverse the trend toward scarcity. Some countries incentivize citizens to use less by offering a cost cut, but if we are going to see the initiatives pay off in a big way, they should really offer corporate savings. If that scenario were to unfold, we would see many more companies like McDonald's Europe getting on board and testing new technologies.

However, we can never underestimate the power of inertia. People tend to ignore the issue of resource scarcity if there is no incentive to reduce water costs and usage. In many communities, water usage is part of the monthly rent or association fees, so some people don't even think about it.

CLIMATE CHANGE

Resource scarcity is directly influenced by climate change. There is no arguing that the world is getting warmer. Or at least it won't be us who will deny it, regardless of the myopia of those who still think of it as a fad. Indeed, 2016 was the hottest year on record. The ocean temperature increased by 1.5 to 2 degrees. As this trajectory continues, the planet is going to change dramatically. It has been suggested that by 2080, the majority of ski resorts in France will cease to exist.[11]

We grow food where the climate, the seasons, and the soil allow us. These factors vary according to what type of crops we are trying to grow and what type of agriculture we practice. There is an expectation that the climate will be somewhat "normal" and behave in accordance with the seasons. We know the seasons will bring certain changes; we're prepared for them, and many farmers rely on them. "Seasonal crops" are an expectation, on a cyclical level, dependent on expected climates.

It is naïve to expect that we will continue to grow food in the same locations and with the same practices we have always used in the face of climate change and global warming in the future. Climate change impacts arable land, growing seasons, dormancy periods, crop viability, and more. If the farmers are not aware of the changes or they don't know how to deal with them, we are looking at a food crisis. Many headlines report lost crops as soon as

---

[11] Benoist Simmat, *Atlas de la France du futur: Notre avenir en 72 cartes* (Paris: Autrement, 2016).

extreme weather conditions hit a specific region. If you live in a country that is dependent on rice or wheat, and one of those crops is wiped out by any of the above-mentioned variables, the population will not have access to basic nutrition, or they will have to import the same product from abroad for a much higher price. Such is the case of rice in Brazil, which is imported from Thailand, every time there is a "bad crop" season.

The good news is we have the ability to address the potentially devastating effects of climate change now before entire countries face starvation or malnutrition. It stands to reason that certain areas that are unarable today will become arable tomorrow. How can we best identify new uses for land and determine where agriculture is shifting? What practices can be implemented—through smart irrigation, crop rotation, or simply a weather forecast? These are questions that can help us capitalize on emerging agricultural opportunities while protecting food sources.

For example, French and Spanish vineyard owners have been actively buying land in the UK and Germany in anticipation of climate change. Although grape growing conditions are not ideal today, eventually, as the planet warms, they will be. It is estimated that by 2050, champagne and Bordeaux would be produced in Britain, while Italy's Chianti will move up north and be produced in

France. Rioja will also be produced north of the Spanish homeland in France.[12] Already, there are quite a few people who are looking ahead and making the necessary investments for future opportunities.

Our hope is that when people engage in a conversation about climate change, they will naturally connect the dots to understand how it will impact food and water availability. As the planet evolves into a new equilibrium, we have the power to guide the evolution of our agricultural models along with it, which is empowering. Rather than thinking about changing tomorrow, we need to focus on changing today.

WASTE

Another current threat to the food supply is waste. Each year, 1.3 billion tons of food—about a third of all that is produced—is wasted, including about 45 percent of all fruits and vegetables, 35 percent of fish and seafood, 30 percent of cereals, 20 percent of dairy products, and 20 percent of meat.[13] Inevitably, food is wasted at the production stage, but a large culprit in food waste is the consumer, particularly within the middle to upper classes. This has

---

12 Ibid.
13 https://www.theguardian.com/environment/2015/aug/12/cutting-food-waste-enough-for-everyone-says-un

been the case throughout history, with the exception of wartime rationing or countries afflicted by famine. In the last several decades, as society has become more prosperous and grown wealthier, we have become more and more wasteful.

We are also wasteful with water even though it is important to us. At the current consumption rate, it is possible that by 2025 two-thirds of the world's population may face water shortages.[14] It is not just a matter of quenching thirst.

Producing food requires a lot of water. For instance, a kilo of beef requires 3,500 liters of water; 460 liters of water is needed for just one kilo of tofu. It takes 120 liters of water to produce just one bottle of wine.[15] That knowledge isn't likely to slow wine consumption, but it is important to be generally aware of how much goes into producing what we often take for granted.

Many companies' value chains would also be deeply affected by water scarcity across regions, but more so where manufacturing is still the key driver of production. An average car containing about 2,150 pounds of steel and 300,000 liters of water is needed to produce the

---

14 http://www.worldwildlife.org/threats/water-scarcity
15 http://waterprint.net

finished steel for just one car.[16] The "waterprint" for a pair of jeans is 11,000 liters of water.[17] Our technological progress might also be hampered: a single computer chip requires 132 liters of clean water to produce.[18]

While the above are only examples, our research exposed us to some absurd requirements for water in our current productive practices, which poses a real problem to how water may become a variable cost for companies capable of undermining profitability.

Water is also needed for sanitation. As cities become ever-more urbanized, the increased requirements on sanitation would put further pressure on the use of water and beyond, in what we see as strings of correlated shortages.

If we continue along the same trajectory we have been following, water is going to be the new oil. It is the single most important natural resource we have on the planet and the most endangered across the spectrum. Even if the richer countries decrease their water consumption, there is still going to be a need for more water on a global level.

---

16 http://www.gracelinks.org/285/the-hidden-water-in-everyday-products
17 http://waterprint.net/jeans.html
18 A. Y. Hoekstra and A. K. Chapagain, "Water Footprints of Nations: Water Use by People as a Function of Their Consumption Pattern," *Water Resource Management* 21, no. 5 (2007): 35–48.

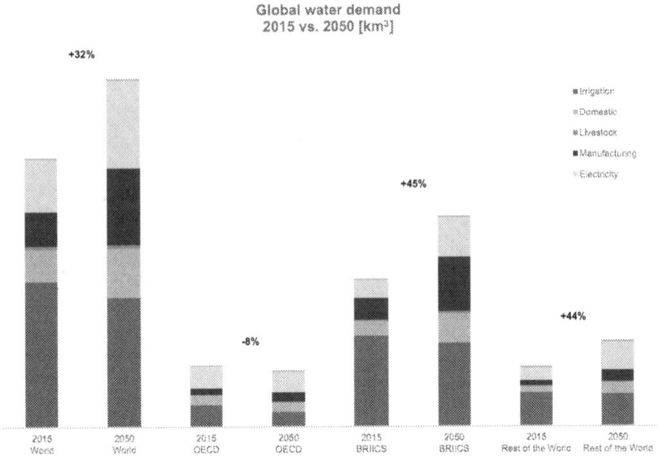

**Global water demand
2015 vs. 2050 [km³]**

- Irrigation
- Domestic
- Livestock
- Manufacturing
- Electricity

+32% (2015 vs 2050 World)
-8% (2015 vs 2050 OECD)
+45% (2015 vs 2050 BRIICS)
+44% (2015 vs 2050 Rest of the World)

BRIICS: Brazil, Russia, India, Indonesia, China and South Africa
Source: Roland Berger, Trend Compendium 2030, November

Some people have a hard time understanding the urgency of this resource scarcity. They say, "Just look at a map of the world! There is more water than land. We have plenty!" The issue is our access to drinkable water does not equal our current rate of consumption and our future needs. We have been taking it for granted that there will always be plenty of water available. In the West, the stuff just pours out of the faucet in abundance, but in India, violence over such liquid gold is on the rise.[19]

Virtually all of our production methods are water intensive, particularly agriculture. Higher life expectancy and larger populations mean we need more water. Emerging

---

19 http://www.reuters.com/article/us-india-water-violence-idUSKCN0ZF0IW

economies need more water to fuel their manufacturing and utilities. Water is at the very core of our existence, and it is the most necessary commodity for development. If we continue along, business as usual, we will hit a wall. When water becomes scarce, everything is impacted. As farming and cattle consumption increases, we are depleting more and more of the land. The price of food will be affected. Lack of water could challenge not only the survival of certain populations but also civilization.

When oil was scarce, paraffin and geo gas were discovered as renewable alternatives. Immediately, the threat diminished, and the price of oil went down. We don't see the same level of sophistication or the potential for alternatives when it comes to water. Of course, it is possible, and we are hopeful, but the tendency toward waste is higher with water than it ever was with oil. Unless we change our view and start to give this endangered resource the credence it so desperately deserves, we're heading for some unpleasant repercussions.

Perhaps if water was treated as a valuable commodity, we would be more mindful of it. Recently, Slovenia declared access to drinkable water a fundamental right for all citizens and stopped it from being commercialized. The country is now trying to pass a law to protect huge amounts of high-quality, clean water that could become the target of foreign and international companies.[20]

THE CIRCULAR ECONOMY

We need to think about how we, as a global community, can use fewer resources along the value chain to prevent depletion. Historically, the price of resources is going up, and we are using more and more of them. The quality of the resources is starting to deteriorate and/or they cost more to extract because the best of the low-hanging fruit has already been plucked.

Currently, there is a strong push for resource protection in Europe, which is traditionally more environmentally conscious than North America. The EU supports the development of a circular economy, which is a way for us to think about slowing down the use of resources. The circular economy is about maintaining the value of products, materials, and resources in the economy for as long as possible and minimizing the generation of waste.

Some may argue these initiatives are not much different than proposing a high-end recycling system, which people have been participating in for years. Recycling is no longer

---

20 https://www.theguardian.com/environment/2016/nov/18/slovenia-adds-water-to-constitution-as-fundamental-right-for-all

a novelty; it is widely practiced and even ingrained in some countries. The issue, however, is not all recycling efforts are equal. Plastic loses its inherent properties every time it is recycled, so a plastic water bottle cannot be recycled into another bottle. Although it is far better to recycle a bottle than to toss it in the trash, the true chemical properties of the plastic are compromised. This method is referred to as open-loop recycling.

If we were to close the loop, which is promoted within a circular economy, we would be able to maintain the integrity of the plastic and reuse it again for the same purpose. The same principle can be applied to almost any resource including copper and gold.

Who pays for the cost of recycling in the current system, or in a future closed-loop program: the consumer, the manufacturer, or the government? The answer varies. In Finland and the United States, for water bottles at least, the manufacturers pay for the cost of their recycling. Modern-day consumers are comforted thinking they are doing something good for the environment by paying a few extra dollars to drink from recycled water bottles, but it's an imperfect system. It's better than nothing, but it could be vastly improved.

There are four elements to the circular economy sphere.

The first is waste reduction. The goal is to reduce *all of the waste*. For example, there is a start-up initiative in the UK called the Real Junk Food Project[21] that engages with supermarkets across the country, leading the way in this arena. The initiative has devised an innovative approach to reuse the fruits and vegetables that are too ugly to be displayed in a retail capacity. Those items may not appear to be perfect on the outside, and they do not meet consumer standards for produce, but they are still edible.

Several supermarket chains that adhered to the project handle this rejected inventory in one of two ways. One, they pass it on directly to their customers at a cheaper price. Instead of discarding the fruit and vegetables, they advertise it by saying, "This fruit is ugly, but it is perfectly edible. Because we bought it at a lower price, so can you." This has been effective in the stores because everyone loves a bargain. Two, they process the ugly produce to create entirely new product lines of soups, shakes, and juices. In this case, they have used the waste to create something of value. They have literally turned waste into food.

The second element within the circular economy is called servitization, which means that instead of selling a

---

21 http://www.telegraph.co.uk/news/2016/09/21/look-inside-the-uks-first-food-waste-supermarket/

product, the product is turned into a service. For example, a Dutch denim company called MUD Jeans rents jeans to customers instead of selling them. The benefit of this is that when the consumer is finished with the jeans, instead of throwing them away, they are returned to the company. The material is reused; therefore, effectively, MUD Jeans is selling a service instead of a product. Ownership creates the sense that you can do whatever you want with a product, including throwing it away, but renting creates a sense of responsibility.

The third element is to lengthen the life span of consumption, which essentially means holding on to things longer. Many products on the market are built for quick obsolescence. Sellers and manufacturers often push us to get a new replacement even though the current product is perfectly good—how many cell phones do you have in your home that you don't use?

Many items are marketed as "disposable," when in fact we should seek items that are "durable." Energy must come from renewable sources. Products that are tossed into the trash heap after one use are of no value whatsoever. It's just a vicious cycle of garbage in and garbage out, and it needs to stop.

The fourth element involves remanufacturing. Car

manufacturers have latched onto this concept by collecting old parts, such as engine blocks and gear boxes, restoring them to almost new condition, and giving those refurbished products a manufacturer's guarantee. They stand by the rebuilt products just as they would brand new parts fresh off the assembly line. The consumer sees a significant cost savings, and it prevents over manufacturing.

More and more companies are starting to think about their products and services through the lens of the circular economy. Inevitably, it will take some time for the idea to fully trickle across the board. Most businesses are still focused exclusively on the bottom line and their profit margins, but slowly, we are starting to see a movement toward resource-saving behaviors.

A WAKE-UP CALL

As discussed in Chapter 3, the world's population is growing. Emerging markets are causing certain populations to get richer and richer, which means they can afford to buy more and consume more. China is a perfect example. After sixty years of living in frugality, a good percentage of people now have more money due to a substantial increase in prosperity. Sadly, many Chinese people engage in extremely wasteful behaviors simply because all of a sudden, they can.

There is a new cultural mindset of waste. In Shanghai, recently, we noticed almost everyone in the restaurant had leftover food on their plates. It seems they overorder on purpose, almost as a signal to show others they can afford to do so. They have no intention of taking the leftovers home with them or giving them to someone else when they leave the restaurant. It is not a stretch to claim that this also happens in other up-and-coming economies.

The car market in China is another good example of this change in behavior. Thirty years ago, the city streets were cluttered with bicycles. Today, those same cities are congested with cars. Most of the people who have cars don't actually need them; they have them just because they can afford them. Emerging countries tend to waste more and recycle less.

In the West, we are seeing the reverse. People are trying to move away from car ownership because it's expensive and, in the cities, largely unnecessary. This is why car sharing and Uber suddenly have vast market dominance. People are looking for alternatives to ownership. Access is far more important.

Some trajectories show that people are paying more attention to how they use resources, but the general population of consumers is going to need more convincing. People are simply not apt to get on board unless there is some clear incentive for them to do so. Even saving a few pennies here and there may not be enough.

For example, the energy companies in the UK have been actively trying to get people to be more aware of their consumption. They have gone so far as to provide each household with a free "smart meter" so everyone knows how much energy they're using and can make adjustments to save money accordingly.

Sadly, the buy-in on this technology is abysmal. Almost no one is using it, because (1) they don't trust the utilities companies, and (2) they don't really care about resource scarcity. It takes too much effort to concentrate on studying the meter to save a few pounds. Most people leave all of their small electronics plugged in, even when they are away on vacation, and don't give it a thought. If we want to change our wasteful behaviors, both the companies that offer the services and the users need to be on board.

The costs of resources are going up, and everything is becoming more expensive in general. At the same time, we are seeing more of our income go to services or products that were previously not critical to survival. Utilities no longer reference water and electricity exclusively. Most people wouldn't be able to function without their cell phones or access to Wi-Fi. Household expenses are going up. We have more things to pay for than just keeping the lights on.

Simultaneously, incomes are not rising at the same level as the "input prices," or utilities. This phenomenon impacts the people at the bottom of the economic spectrum far more than it does the people at the top. We will cover this in depth when we discuss inequalities in the next chapter, but like everything within DRIVE, it is all interconnected.

Resources are impacted by demographics and social changes, and the distribution of resources leads to inequalities among populations. If we are spending considerably more on our daily utilities, will we have enough to live those longer lives we're projected to live?

CHAPTER 5

I: INEQUALITIES

For centuries, the distribution of wealth has been a core topic of many economic debates and writings. Colonization and its practices drove a permanent wedge in communities and only reinforced the divide between the haves and the have-nots. The division continues to widen as the world population grows.

After World War II, much of North America, Europe, and Japan saw a population explosion with the birth of the baby boomers. In the United States alone, it grew at an average rate of 26 percent from 1949 to 1959.[1] A "parental model" of economics was applicable to these regions, in which 80 percent of the global resources were controlled by 30 percent of the population.

---
1   http://www.cdc.gov/nchs/products/vsus.htm

In the United States, the top 1 percent earned more than 21 percent of the country's total income in 2013.² In fact, the top 1 percent has almost as much wealth as the bottom 90 percent. In China, the richest 1 percent of households owns a third of the country's wealth. By contrast, the poorest 25 percent of Chinese households own just 1 percent of the country's total wealth.³

There are several different layers of inequality beyond just the obvious monetary differences between the rich and the poor. Those levels are dictated by realistic factors, such as access to resources, as well as the *type of access* people have to resources. The structure of inequalities is varied and complex, simply because there are so many layers. For the purpose of our discussion, inequalities are defined as unequal access to multiple streams of resources and this goes beyond financial resources.

We cannot talk about inequalities without also talking about demographics, social changes, and resources. Those elements impact distribution and how the economy evolves or develops. *D* and *R* are macrophenomenal in that they happen on a very large scale. We noticed that the consequences of *D* and *R* are particularly impactful for those who are on the wrong side of their evolution. The

---

2   http://inequality.org/income-inequality/
3   https://www.ft.com/content/3c521faa-baa6-11e5-a7cc-280dfe875e28

people who pay the highest prices are the ones who are already suffering from the growing imbalances.

INCOME INEQUALITY

The core difference between rich and poor is cash, although cash is only the tip of the iceberg. The rise of the top 1 percent, particularly within the last thirty to forty years, is a popular media topic. The rich get rich and the poor get poorer, especially in the United States and in Europe. However, emerging economies in China, India, and other countries with social welfare issues are seeing the same trends. People within these populations have become important players and vocal advocates for increased economic growth policies in their regions. More and more, wealth is distributed to an increasingly smaller number of people. The attention of renowned scholars in the past decade demonstrates how distributed the phenomenon is becoming.

The word *wealth* does not apply exclusively to cash on hand. It encompasses all the financial elements of an individual's monetary value including personal and company assets, investments, returns, and anything else that brings money in. Compared to today's ratio of 99:1, the Pareto principle—or the 80/20 rule[4] of distribution—from the

---

4   http://www.investopedia.com/terms/p/paretoprinciple.asp

late 1800s looks downright luxurious. Income inequality only serves to perpetuate the top 1 percent problem.

The people with real power have nothing to lose. Everyone in society is impacted over the long-term. Look at consumption as an example. Joseph Stiglitz, a world-renowned economist, writes:

> Consider someone like Mitt Romney, whose income in 2010 was £21.7 million. Even if Romney chose to live a much more indulgent lifestyle, he would spend only a fraction of that sum in a typical year to support himself and his wife in their several homes. But take the same amount of money and divide it among 500 people—say, in the form of jobs paying $43,400 apiece—and you'll find that almost all the money gets spent. The relationship is straightforward and ironclad: as more money becomes concentrated at the top, aggregate demand goes into a decline.[5]

Perhaps worse is, even the top 1 percent is no longer fashionable—0.1 percent is the new 1 percent. It appears that more and more of our economies are accrued to the top 0.1 percent. The highest 0.1 percent of income earners in the United States, accounting for almost 5 percent of the national income, have over recent decades seen their

---

5 http://www.vanityfair.com/news/2012/05/joseph-stiglitz-the-price-on-inequality

incomes rise much faster than the rest of the top 1 percent.[6] These families now own roughly the same share of wealth as the bottom 90 percent.[7]

Yet, at the same time, while the top 0.1 percent owns more than 20 percent of total wealth, the top 0.01 percent hold 10 percent of the total.[8] Apparently, this is another worrying trend in terms of income gap.[9,10] So, while at first the cover title of an issue of the *Economist* "America's New Aristocracy" seems like an oxymoron—especially for a country that stresses the importance of meritocracy—the description is becoming more appropriate.[11] The imbalance of wealth distribution is a rising concern. We find it interesting to note the 1 percent phenomenon does not occur in dictatorships; only elected democracies experience this and at the concerning rate we have just described. Income equality is just one level within inequalities. There are many other factors at play within this discussion.

---

6 http://inequality.org/income-inequality/
7 Emmanuel Saez and Gabriel Zucman, "Wealth Inequality in the United States since 2013: Evidence from Capitalized Income Tax Data," NBER Working Paper 20625, 2014.
8 http://inequality.org/wealth-inequality/
9 http://www.cnbc.com/2014/03/31/the-other-wealth-gapthe-1-vs-the-001.html
10 https://www.bloomberg.com/view/articles/2015-09-10/the-top-0-01-another-wealth-gap-matters-more
11 "America's New Aristocracy," *Economist*, January 24, 2015.

The gap is only getting wider, and wherever there is a gap, there is a cost. Who is paying the highest price for the rise of inequalities? What do increasing inequalities say for the prospects of our younger generations? There is a vicious cycle at play, particularly for the middle class. Those at the top will continue to thrive at the top, but those at the bottom or in the middle must work all that much harder to get to the top, if they can get there at all.

A report in 2014 points out that 7 percent of the UK's children attend private schools (with annual fees around £15,000 or $18,600 US). Yet, they account for a disproportional share of what are considered the best jobs in Britain. Almost 65 percent of the people surveyed believe "who you know" is more important than "what you know," and three-quarters of the people think family background has a significant influence on life chances in Britain today.[12]

It certainly doesn't help that wealth perpetuates among those who are intellectually privileged, especially in our knowledge-based economy. Far more than in previous generations, clever, successful men marry clever, successful women. Such "assortative mating" increases inequality by 25 percent as two-degree households typically enjoy

---

12 Alan Milburn, *Elitist Britain?* (London: Social Mobility and Child Poverty Commission, 2014).

two large incomes.[13] Power couples conceive bright children and bring them up in stable homes. Only 9 percent of college-educated mothers who give birth each year are unmarried, compared with 61 percent of high school dropouts.[14]

Middle- and lower-class individuals receive fewer educational opportunities than the upper class, further widening the gap. Children from wealthy families are found to be more intellectually developed than those with less, because they are exposed to more at a younger age. An earlier study has found that children in professional families heard on average 2,100 words an hour. On the other hand, those from the working class heard 1,200 words an hour, whereas those whose families lived on welfare heard only 600. Putting it differently, by the age of three, children from the privileged families would have heard 45 million words, some 20 million more than those from working-class families and 30 million more than those from welfare families.[15] One's background defines what will happen down the road.

---

13 Jeremy Greenwood, Nezih Guner, Georgi Kocharkov, and Cezar Santos, "Marry Your Like: Assortative Mating and Income Inequality," NBER Working Paper 19829, January 2014.

14 http://www.economist.com/news/leaders/21640331-importance-intellectual-capital-grows-privilege-has-become-increasingly

15 Betty Hart and Todd R. Risley, "The Early Catastrophe: The 30 Million Word Gap by Age 3," *American Educator* 27, no. 1 (2003): 4–9.

Education is starting to play a big role in inequalities, especially in the United States. The rising cost of education makes it cost prohibitive for many. Affluent children have a higher probability of attending and being able to pay for good schools, which will lead to better earning opportunities when they start their careers.

The college admission process alone is completely overwhelming. It typically requires some guidance from a parent who has been there before and knows the ropes. People who come to the process from working families have an almost insurmountable hill to climb. Plus, those who cannot afford to pay the tuition up front take on massive amounts of debt, which puts them even further behind the eight ball. New generations of young people are starting their careers tens of thousands of dollars in the hole.

Richer people are also privileged in another way. They live longer than poorer ones. The top 10 percent live an average of twelve years longer than the poorest tier for men and almost eight years more for women.[16] Indeed, income inequality has inflicted costs on all facets of our social lives. Inequalities have a direct correlation with many social issues including mental health, drug use, physical

---

16   Barry P. Bosworth and Kathleen Burke, *Differential Mortality and Retirement Benefits in the Health and Retirement Study* (Chestnut Hill, MA: Center for Retirement Research at Boston College, 2014).

health, obesity, educational performance, teenage births, violence, imprisonment, punishment, and social mobility. It has been found that the higher the income inequality within a country, the worse these problems are.[17]

CAPITAL INEQUALITY

A discussion about capital is most usefully conducted in terms of the real economy versus the financial economy. Simplistically, in a real economy, growth is relevant to the effort you are willing to put in. For example, if you want to create value, you need to work. You need people, or land, or resources to make things in exchange for cash. This represents a "normal" exchange of labor or resources and the subsequent benefits. You work for X and then you get Y in return, which is the basic premise of trade.

In a financial economy, the coefficient is very different, and it can be exponential. You can have a certain amount of money parked in the bank, and that money will grow on its own, without any work on your behalf. The value increases by its own resources. This is what we call making money out of money.

Those who do not own capital must go to work. In the old

---

17 Richard Wilkinson and Kate Pickett, *The Spirit Level: Why Equality Is Better for Everyone* (London: Allan Lane, 2009).

model, workers were the most productive engines of the economy, but they are becoming the most redundant in the new model, especially one based on automation. They also represent the largest part of the population.

Can you see how the two economies might be at odds with each other and create inequalities? On the one hand, we have an economy that creates wealth only through an exchange of labor, land, and capital. On the other hand, we have an economy that creates wealth only by increasing what was already there to begin with. There is no trade-off.

Capital grows at a much slower rate in the real economy than it does in the financial economy, owned and controlled largely by the top 1 percent, which loops us back to the income inequality conversation. The imbalance is about the relationship between who owns the capital and how it is distributed.

The questions surrounding income inequalities and the problems they present have been a concern for some time now. Recently, the French economist Thomas Piketty supercharged the conversation in his book, *The Economics of Inequality*.[18] Through historical data, he shows that the growth on the return of capital is bigger than the growth

---

18 Thomas Piketty, *Capital in the Twenty-First Century* (Cambridge, MA: Harvard University Press, 2014).

of return on the economy. Basically, those who have the money to make money are going to fare far better than those who get money from working in return for their labor. In a nutshell, the benefits of investing outweigh the benefits of work. His observations are not new, but he did bring attention to the issues and raised concerns.

Where does the capital made from capital go, anyway? If someone makes a profit off an investment, what is he or she likely to spend it on? Usually, the money is reinvested through any number of financial instruments available, such as real estate, stocks and bonds, savings accounts, trust funds for the grandkids, and tax-free and charitable donations. These expenditures, although gratifying on a personal level, don't do too much for society as a whole.

The prosperity of any society depends on its ability to be productive. Or at least, productivity is the mechanism that generates value in our society. Money is needed to fuel activities, institutions, and infrastructures that promote productivity. If the wealthy and/or the government don't invest in these areas, the economy slows down, which means it is no longer profitable. Therefore, it is in everyone's best interest, including the wealthy, to support the real economy.

Some people argue that it doesn't matter as long as the

pie is getting bigger and bigger. But we find this view to be wrong. Not everyone's share of the economic pie is growing. Two groups are most likely to see their slices supersized: (1) those who own nonhuman assets (such as equipment, structures, intellectual property, financial assets, and capital), and (2) those who have special human assets (in the form of talents, training, education, experience, and skills).[19]

We existed in a different paradigm when the financial economy was less sophisticated and things moved at a slower pace. Government worked to protect its citizens and preserve a certain way of life. Today, the activities or policies we think will benefit everyone seem to inadvertently benefit the upper crust above everyone else. This is perhaps best captured by a phrase from economist Joseph Stiglitz: "Of the 1 percent, by the 1 percent, for the 1 percent."[20]

Capital inequalities exist according to reverse logistics. We work hard; we strive to be productive and fiscally diligent. We pay attention to politics and try to elect officials who will best serve our needs and the needs of our children.

---

19 Erik Brynjolfsson and Andrew McAfee, *Race against the Machine: How the Digital Revolution Is Accelerating Innovation, Driving Productivity, and Irreversibly Transforming Employment and the Economy* (Lexington, MA: Digital Frontier Press, 2012).

20 http://www.vanityfair.com/news/2011/05/top-one-percent-201105

Yet, whatever they propose or advocate, regardless of good intentions, does not necessarily help the middle or lower segments of society. This is precisely why the old models for creating value are inadequate today. If we continue along the same path we are on right now, inequalities will be a certain trajectory.

There is always someone who is making exponentially more than the rest of the pack. In this era of capital abundance, there has never been so much currency floating through the global economic system. A select few hold the purse strings, quite literally, for the rest of the world, and there will be important repercussions. The middle class is rapidly shrinking, debts are soaring higher than ever, and the rich watch their piles of cash continue to grow.

Many governments favor capital holders above anyone else in society. Just look at what happened during the financial crisis of 2008 in the United States. When the big banks started to go belly-up due primarily to negligence and greed, the government stepped in with a check (from the taxpayers, no less) to save the banks from themselves. At the same time, as a result of the banks' gross malpractices, the average American Joe taxpayers lost their homes in droves. This scenario is a perfect example of government-supported inequalities. They were unwilling to help the regular people, and yet they were willing to prop up the very institutions that got everyone into the mess to begin with.

It's easy to point a finger at the United States because the experience is fresh. The world waited to see how government would handle the economic collapse and what the ripple effects would be. Other world governments followed the United States' lead. Most banks in the world are propped up by government money.

In the face of worldwide recession, governments looked for ways to give the economy a boost. They wanted to make sure there was enough money to lend small- and medium-sized enterprises (SMEs), which make up 60-70 percent of economic activity and people who are hired.[21] It makes sense that governments would want to ensure the economic viability of this market segment, because it represents the majority of their people. Typically, the way this works is, governments print money—quantitative easing—and give it to the banks to lend out.

The only problem with this plan is, most recently, the banks decided to hold on to the money. They did this for two reasons. One, risk management decisions are under close scrutiny due to the banks' previous indiscretions

---

21 International Labour Office (ILO), *Small and Medium-Sized Enterprises and Decent and Productive Employment Creation* (Geneva: ILO, 2015).

with rampant loaning. Lending out money is risky now because there are increased compliance laws and regulations. Two, the banks prefer to use the money for themselves. Over time, they can use that government money to repair their own rotten balance sheets.

Regardless of the government's intent, it backfired. The banks aren't lending, and the SMEs aren't borrowing. If they did borrow, it would cost them an arm and a leg in interest fees. Plus, printing extra money causes inflation. Who bears the brunt of inflation? Everyone. Even if we had nothing whatsoever to do with the financial crisis, as taxpayers, we are all still paying for their behavior.

What have the banks done since the big bailout of 2008? It would be a stretch to say they learned their lesson and have righted their ways. Standards are slippery where banks are concerned. They are both the keepers of the money and the makers of the money. Capital inequalities are very much alive and spiraling ever further out of reach from the regular Joes.

In many ways, the government has been operating on behalf of the banks. Unlike the United States and, to a lesser extent, the UK, companies in continental Europe and Japan rely far more on lending than sharing equity to finance their businesses. This matters, a lot, in fact.

Current accounting rules allow companies to pay interest on debt before they pay corporate taxes. The more debt they have, the lower their taxable income. The result is that companies load themselves up with debt. Lenders, including the banks, make more profit. Governments, on the other hand, receive less tax income.

In 2007, the annual value of the forgone tax revenues in Europe was around 3 percent of GDP (US$510 billion). In the United States, the loss was equivalent to almost 5 percent of GDP (US$725 billion).[22] To put this into context, Britain and the Eurozone spent more on this so-called senseless subsidy than on defense.[23]

Put differently, governments are using taxpayers' money to serve the interests of investors in banks, effectively transferring public funds to capital holders. And governments often have no choice but to bail banks out, simply because the fall of one bank might set off a chain reaction that could decimate the fundamentals of our economy. From bank investors' perspectives, their money is, to a large extent, backed up, if not safeguarded, by taxpayers' money.

Without abolishing this rule, the loss in tax incomes will

---

22 "The Great Distortion," *Economist*, May 16, 2015.
23 "A Senseless Subsidy," *Economist*, May 16, 2015.

continue. Yet, in the wake of the financial crisis, governments in various countries chose to boost their coffers by raising value-added tax (VAT) and cutting back on personal income tax benefits. It seems they would rather punish taxpayers and keep benefiting borrowing companies.

Europe's preference for debt over shares is doing its economy a great disservice. It is not promoting the right dynamics for new business creation. By nature, lenders only have to worry about covering the downside risk (i.e., bankruptcy); they are concerned only with interest paid and loans repaid. The borrowers' success does not matter to the lenders. By contrast, shareholders lose money when things go wrong. Yet, shareholders are attracted by the potentially unlimited upside gain. This comparison may sound prosaic, but the consequences are rather profound.

This "inequality of mood" is important for promoting a more entrepreneurial and innovation-driven economy. As such, an economy requires investors to take risks and potential losses to be spread among investors.[24] Risk capital is a key source of funding for the realization of novel technologies and ideas.

---

24 We like to thank Xavier Rolet, CEO of the London Stock Exchange Group, for the idea of "inequality of mood."

"As long as a broader set of European investors don't lose their aversion to risk capital and create more funds for early-stage companies, it is unlikely that Europe will be able to sufficiently grow existing dynamic start-up hubs like London, Berlin, and Stockholm, or meaningfully support entrepreneurship in many other cities across the continent," said Philippe Cerf, a managing director looking after the technology, media, and telecommunications' practice of Credit Suisse.[25]

Whereas both the companies and lenders gain from the increased amount of debt available, this is not necessarily the case for individuals. They cannot write off their debt, which only serves to deepen the inequalities between the haves and the have-nots. If you are the head of a household with $20,000 of credit card debt, there are no loopholes, and there are no shortcuts to profit. Your only option is to pay until there is nothing left to pay, with interest. Who said life was fair?

People are under the delusion that we are living better now than we were, for example, in the 1970s. It may appear that way, and we think we can afford more than we did back then, but the truth is, most people live off their credit cards. If you happen to be one of those rare individuals who pay their bills on time for a few months in a row, the

---
25 Interview with Philippe Cerf, March 3, 2016.

credit card company will reward you with an even higher credit limit. Buying on credit is nowhere near the same as buying with cash, and it doesn't take long for those balances to add up.

The basic idea behind credit cards is to delay payment for a few days or weeks. The psychological component of the credit card promotes the illusion you can afford something, when the truth is, most people can't. It gives consumers a false sense of affordability. This predicament has made the middle class even more vulnerable than it was back in the 1970s when people largely paid for things with cash or a check. These days, both of those payment methods are becoming obsolete.

The housing and mortgage crisis in the United States, which coincided with the banking crisis in 2008, was due in part to an inflated (and false) sense of affordability. Anyone with a driver's license and a Social Security number could get a bank loan for a mortgage. In the 1990s and up to the early 2000s, it was possible to get 100 percent financing with zero dollars down.

This scenario wasn't only true for working professionals with fixed incomes. It was also true for people who already carried a tremendous amount of debt through student loans and who were just getting started in their careers.

In many cases, loans were given to new immigrants without any income whatsoever, let alone a command of the language or an understanding of complicated banking practices. These approvals only perpetuated the perception of affordability. It encouraged people to buy things they could not afford and likely would never be able to afford.

And then what happened? The banks moved in to foreclose. They repossessed the property, and people lost their homes. Not only did they lose their shelter, but they also lost their life savings, their self-esteem, and their hope for a piece of the American dream. Clearly, the risk of the loan was not shared between the bank and the individual. As soon as the person defaulted in a payment, the bank won. The bank simply took back the asset, and again, the gap widened.

Insurance companies work in much the same way. The people with money convince those without money to give them the little bit they have. In the case of housing loans, the banks sell people on the American dream of home ownership. In the case of insurance companies, they sell them on fear. This practice has become ingrained in some cultures so much so that it is "normal" for people of very little means to surrender a percentage of their earnings in exchange for a sense of protection. Insurance safeguards against the fear of illness, accidents, and even death.

A further example of inequalities still exists within the real estate market in terms of housing values. A recent example references price inflation across states in the United States. Housing prices in California are notoriously very high. In many cases, owning property is not an option because the prices, particularly along the coast, are exorbitant. If you want to buy a house for a family of four, you can expect to pay at least a million dollars.

Many people decided they could not afford to buy houses in California, but if they drove to Arizona, they could get the same size house for $250,000 as opposed to $1,000,000. For a working family, this scenario was far more affordable. Then, someone from California would drive by and offer $350,000 in cash for the same house. Suddenly, the house was off the market at an inflated price. This happened over and over to the point where the Arizona housing market was distorted.

The Californians who sucked up the houses in Arizona were still getting a better price on their inventory than they would have if they had bought at home. Because they had more capital to begin with, they could tip the entire market in their favor. This practice has since been made illegal, but it is a great example of a perfectly functioning market that is recalibrated according to individual income and capital distribution.

These are the mechanics by which inequalities are exacerbated. They are part and parcel of a systematic, worldwide issue of imbalance between resources at every level. No matter what lens you look through—housing, banking, employment, or education—the system favors the upper echelon. It's no wonder we are witnessing the demise of the middle class. Given today's ever-widening parameters, it's hard to see it regaining ground.

AGE INEQUALITY

In addition to income and capital inequality, another "time bomb" is age inequality. This does not refer to discrimination against the elderly. On the contrary, the older generations are enjoying considerably more than the younger generations.

They have more advantages, more luxuries, and more entitlements than the millennials and generation Z are likely to ever see—at this rate, anyway. There are a lot of perks to being old today. Indeed, in the UK, young people have suffered a drop in income since the Great Recession of 2008. Yet, old people have enjoyed a big rise in the

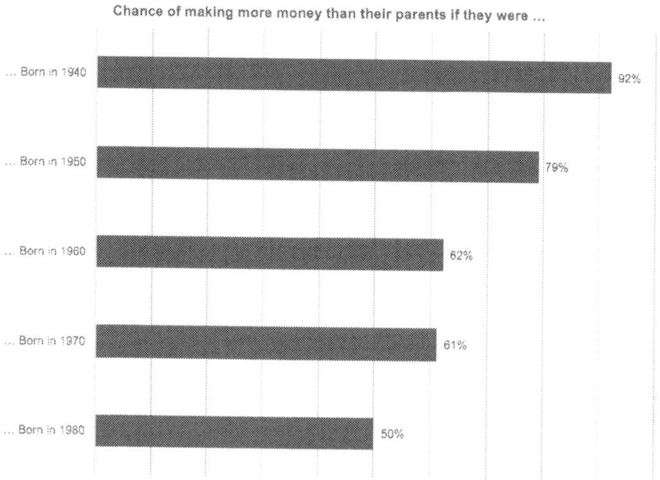

Chance of making more money than their parents if they were ...

- ... Born in 1940: 92%
- ... Born in 1950: 79%
- ... Born in 1960: 62%
- ... Born in 1970: 61%
- ... Born in 1980: 50%

Source: https://www.nytimes.com/2016/12/08/opinion/the-american-dream-quantified-at-last.html?_r=0

past seven years, so much so that seniors are now the least likely group to be experiencing income poverty.[26] A recent study in the United States shows that a decreasing number of young people are expecting to be as financially well-off as their parents.

It's curious, if not sad, that many people and companies are more interested in understanding how young people work and spend, so as to push more goods and services on them. "We are frequently bombarded by information and advice about how to understand the millennial generation. But personally, I'm suspicious of efforts to stereotype and generalize about individuals and their

[26] Chris Belfield, Jonathan Cribb, Andrew Hood, and Robert Joyce, *The Big Challenge on Living Standards Is to Boost Incomes for Those in Work* (London: Institute for Fiscal Studies, July 2016).

circumstances and motivations," said Gavin Devine, CEO of Newgate Communications, a corporate communications and public relations firm. He further adds, "And then there are endless reports explaining that the millennials like to share, require constant praise, and so forth. But I find much of what is written about them to be patronizing and infantilizing. A much bigger problem—finding them job opportunities—deserves grown-up answers."[27]

The job market for the young generation is more competitive than it has ever been. Not only do our kids have more people to contend with, but there are also fewer vacancies available because people are retiring later. At the same time, there are fewer jobs because of technology and the rise of artificial intelligence. Also, it costs more to make ends meet. Many young professionals share housing to cover living expenses.

In the UK and throughout the EU, labor policies favor the older workforce. The youngest people are usually fired first, while the older workers can stay on and collect their paychecks. The law is on the side of people who already have jobs, which does not help the economy, necessarily. Young people have the fresh ideas and the energy to drive home new initiatives, but the older people are protected, even if they do tend to fall asleep at the wheel.

---
27 Interview with Gavin Devine, February 10, 2016.

Youth unemployment is a real problem in the EU and in many places. Globally, youth unemployment is on the rise.[28] We refer to it as the new brain drain. For example, coffee shops in the UK are staffed primarily by Italians and Spaniards in their twenties. This is a strange phenomenon because Spain has the highest percentage of graduates with higher degrees. However, Spanish and Italian labor laws are so rigid and the job markets are so stagnant that their young people are not able to get jobs. They graduate from university, move to the UK, obtain low-paying positions to tide themselves over, and then launch their careers on non-native soil.

Spain and Italy are losing their best and brightest at record rates. It's even crazier because the government pays for higher education in those countries. Effectively, they are paying to train their youth to go work abroad. It makes absolutely no sense.

Aside from government regulations, there are other factors at work as well. For example, industry requirements and needs are shifting dramatically. Twenty years ago, if someone wanted to become a doctor in the United States, he or she would accumulate approximately $300,000–$350,000 in debt. Between undergraduate, med school,

---

28 http://www.ilo.org/global/about-the-ilo/newsroom/news/ WCMS_513728/ lang--en/index.htm

and residency, the price tag was pretty steep. After ten years of practicing medicine, it was feasible that a person would have paid off his or her debt, and the rest of his or her salary was gravy.

Let's say that the same person wanted to become a doctor today. He or she would face an entirely different landscape. For starters, the price tag on the debt would be much higher. Certified nurses who require less training have replaced many doctors' jobs in hospitals. They can usually become certified in twenty-two months or less, but they are still highly specialized and qualified. There is no guarantee that the med school graduate will be able to secure a well-paid position, let alone pay off his or her med school loans after ten years. What used to be a safe bet and a good risk has become an uncertain, impossible risk to manage.

In the past, the price of education was meant to justify employability. These days, an expensive education can't even guarantee employment. Now we are faced with a population of smart, well-educated people who cannot find a way forward. The inequality has expanded beyond blue versus white collar; it is happening across industries and borders, without any order whatsoever. There is, however, opportunity within the *I*. We can change entitlements, the tuition structure, the culture of debt, and the way we view private property. We have to, because the old assumptions no longer hold water.

TECHNOLOGICAL INEQUALITY

Since the mid-1980s, the middle-income group has been gradually disappearing. Even though the real GDP per capita and output per person are going up, median family income in the United States has been shrinking.[29] Just as worrying is common in sixteen European countries, including some with very different social contrasts than that of the United States, the middle-income group has seen the most number of jobs vanishing.[30]

The reason is that digitization, automation, and technology have replaced a good percentage of the workforce. With advances in artificial intelligence and robotics, this trend is only going to continue, and there are many implications. Traditionally, technology has had a significant impact on manual laborers. These days, an algorithm is encroaching on white-collar jobs as well. It seems no one is safe from being replaced by the almighty machines. Experts project that at least 47 percent of jobs will be

---

29 Amy Bernstein and Anand Raman, "The Great Decoupling: An Interview with Erik Brynjolfsson and Andrew McAfee," *Harvard Business Review*, June 2015.

30 Maarten Goos, Alan Manning, and Anna Salomons, "Explaining Job Polarization: Routine-Biased Technological Change and Offshoring," *American Economic Review* 104, no. 8 (2014): 2509-26.

replaced by technology.[31] In a recent interview with a global bank, the CFO told us that a major finance function is currently in the process of shedding 80 percent of personnel, all of which will be absorbed by computers. Whereas the employees can be losing out, the real winners are the tech and software providers.

With the rise of new algorithms and robotics, many jobs are doomed to disappear. Yet, capital investors will reap huge rewards on such occasion. Someone in the United States came up with software that basically replaces many functions of accounting, which is yet another traditional white-collar industry. Of course, the person who created the software is a billionaire, but thousands of highly trained professional accountants are out of work.[32]

More jobs are disappearing that we thought would have had greater staying power. For example, ten years ago, it was understood and expected that someone with a recently minted PhD in finance from a top business school could easily find a good paying job as a "quant guy"—someone who could crunch complex mathematical financial models—at any bank. Exactly ten years later, anyone with a degree of the same caliber would be lucky

---

31 http://www.bbc.com/future/story/20150805-will-machines-eventually-take-on-every-job
32 Erik Brynjolfsson and Andrew McAfee, *The Second Machine Age: Work, Progress, and Prosperity in a Time of Brilliant Technologies* (New York: Norton, 2014).

to find a back-office job. Computerized algorithms have swiftly replaced quantitative analysis professionals.

The insurance industry is feeling the heat, too. In the past, when an accident was reported, the insurance company would send a loss adjuster to the scene to evaluate the extent of the damages and assess the value of the payout. The work was incredibly subjective and required detailed assessments and thorough opinions.

These days, insurance companies are moving away from using adjusters particularly for smaller property claims. If they are faced with a big incident, such as a major flood or an oil well blowout, they resort to human beings. But for other more recurring low-value events, the assessments of claims are increasingly made by machines. "This is especially the case when risk of a claim has been improved by data analytics that lead to a better prediction of outcomes and decision making. Thus, we need fewer but better qualified multidisciplinary loss adjusters than before," said Clive Nicholls, UK and Ireland CEO of Crawford & Company, the world's largest independent provider of claims management solutions to insurance companies and self-insured entities.[33]

---

33 Interview with Clive Nicholls, March 25, 2016.

Income equality is not just about the rich getting richer; it's also about the middle losing ground and the poor getting poorer. It often has no correlation to the wealth of a particular government. Humans are not favored to win the battle against the machines. This is not a sci-fi movie; it is real! Technology favors those who come up with the ideas, and humans are known to make errors. The more advanced the technological infrastructure of an industry, the higher its productivity and the less reliant it is on a human workforce, which is why there are fewer jobs available than ever before. If anything, technology is only going to accelerate the pace of change.

POLITICAL INEQUALITY

Of all the elements within DRIVE, inequalities are the scariest. While people seem genuinely interested in understanding the mechanics and interconnectedness of *D* and *R,* and even *V* and *E,* not everyone has the same level of engagement in *I*. Those at the top are perfectly happy where they are, and people tend to get prickly when you start talking about wealth redistribution. As Stiglitz notes, even though the US economy grew significantly during the first six years of George W. Bush's administration, "the growth helped people who had no need of any help, and failed to help those who need plenty."[34] A rising tide

---

34 http://www.vanityfair.com/news/2007/12/bush200712

lifted all yachts, but there are many people who are just hanging on to floating planks and holey rafts.

The only people who have any real power to make changes as far as inequalities are concerned are the politicians. Politicians, unlike the rest of the world, are not in danger of being replaced by machines. At the same time, many companies that are big enough and rich enough have the financial power to lobby for policies that are in their favor. Money and politics have a long history of getting into bed with each other. It's one of the few things that have not changed over the past several decades.

Three of the 2016 US presidential candidates came from families with deep American political ties. Whoever won would have to face the wife of a former president. And in the end, it was a billionaire who became the next president. Political clout—like bloodline or wealth—is becoming an inherited trait. What chance does the average Joe stand against someone who represents nothing short of a dynasty?

The money will stay at the top because businesses need their initiatives pushed through so they can make more money. They need the politicians to pull the policy-making strings and keep the wheels of commerce spinning.

People have a tendency to overlook inequalities or divisions. We are used to it as a part of life. Shortly after the Brexit referendum, the media started using the term *the great divide*, as if it was new or unexpected. On the contrary, the "divide" has been around as long as the conversation. It didn't just spring up when it was time to go to the polls.

Whether we are talking about the UK or the United States, the world is moving toward free trade and globalization. All of the policies and movements that support these initiatives inherently benefit certain sections of society: the well-off segment. Inevitably, just by the nature of the beast, whenever someone wins, some else must lose. The people on the losing side have always been there, voicing their opinions.

For example, London does not represent all of Britain, as we so vividly just learned. There are many towns north of London that were vibrant at the height of industrialism but have fallen derelict, like Detroit in the United States. Manufacturing towns have gone belly-up because of foreign trade.

Because people have lost their income, they need to file for government-sponsored benefits. Then they are stigmatized by the very people who made the decision to export.

In many ways, these people are stuck. They've lost their way of life, the pride of their work, and a purpose.

It is not hard to understand why many of these towns voted to leave the EU and London voted to remain. The same goes for the US presidential election. Globalization and the policies that support it help the people who have been educated, who earn a nice wage, and who live in a posh city, not those whose interests have been overlooked or ignored. There are many angry people out there who feel left out as the world marches on without them.

Politicians are far removed from ordinary people and their needs. They are accustomed to capitalizing on the challenges regular people face as a means to advance their own agendas. To that end, Brexit is a fascinating example of political inequality flipped on its head in response to wealth inequality.

Inequalities are not without consequences, and other countries should heed the wake-up call to close the gap. When one segment of the population is ignored and disenfranchised, they will rise up and bite. In the UK and the United States, it was with an election, but in many other cases throughout history, it has been through violence.

The Middle East is another well-known region of unrest

and volatility. Throughout history, it has endured invasion from all directions. The Brits, the French, the Italians, and their Asian and African neighbors have conquered and divided the territory more times than many scholars and nationalists can keep up with. Where does it begin and where does it end? The people of the Middle East have the added strain of religious inequality—with multiple warring factions and sects—on top of political and social unrest. These factors contribute to why efforts at unification have been unsuccessful. There are too many issues at play.

Throughout history, the weak have traditionally leveraged their position by creating monsters worse than themselves. Allies quickly morph into antagonists when the climate is ripe for upheaval. Division creates impact, and although it is not always intentional, it certainly is effective. There is an entire nomenclature for division which is ultimately designed to divide and conquer: north vs. south, black vs. white, men vs. women, EU vs. Britain, the haves vs. the have-nots. We have seen it in the UK with Brexit, the United States with Trump's presidential run, China with nationalism, and the Middle East with continued terrorist sects. They are all a direct result of inequalities throughout the society.

NOW WHAT?

It may seem as if these tensions rise out of nowhere, but the fact is, the tensions have been boiling for decades. The systems we have in place are no longer working for the majority of people, and the discontent is emerging—louder perhaps than in the past and through new channels and on new platforms. More often than not, these voices are clamoring for justice.

The inequalities that exist throughout the world tell a story. When we can open our eyes and minds, we are able to see the divisions more clearly. There is no use crying over spilled milk and bemoaning current events. The best course forward is to examine what is happening around us through the DRIVE framework. From today forward, there are many factors to take into account, such as automation and how it will continue to impact us, as well as the inevitable rise of the robots. We need to look closely at the specific technologies we know are going to last so we can evolve with them.

When you can forecast something, you can also backcast it, which is useful for examining a current situation. For example, income equality has always existed, and the gap will continue to widen. Capital tends to be concentrated in big cities because that's where the rich people live and do business. That's also where they will continue to live and work. Technology has been replacing the workforce for decades, and that, too, will continue.

Because we look at the world through the DRIVE lens, we are less surprised by events when they happen. Although we would not necessarily have been able to predict Brexit twenty years ago, the framework would certainly suggest that not just the UK but many societies would have a rocky transition into the twenty-first century. The event itself was not evident, but there were some overarching structures and systems unfolding to create tension. While pockets of their own countrymen were alienated and left to their own devices, the British government is seen by many within the country to have demonstrated carelessness around benefits and entitlements that were allocated to foreigners. Like adding fuel to the fire, the trend toward globalization and urbanization only exacerbates inequalities, which is one of the biggest challenges any country faces.

When Theresa May stepped in as prime minister, the very first thing she declared was making Britain "a country that works for everyone." She immediately sent a clear message that one of the primary drivers behind Brexit was the inequality throughout the country. What she plans to do about it is another story. How will she move the needle?

Only time will tell how her leadership will either further drive the country apart or bring it together.

To have a truly productive conversation on the matter, we need to include the international community. If someone is without a job in northern England, that person's circumstances are likely linked to a trade agreement in China, or a factory worker in the Czech Republic, or even a manufacturing plant in India.

We need to have international reflection about how to generate value in our own economies and how to hold on to it or distribute it, or both. How can we best incentivize our citizens? Where are the discrepancies? How can we lessen the divide? How and where can we come together? DRIVE needs to become a universal way of looking at the problem(s), so that together, we look at the issues through the same lens.

PART 3

HARNESSING THE POWER OF HOPE

CHAPTER 6
V: VOLATILITY, SCALE, AND COMPLEXITY

Due to rapidly changing technological developments, we are experiencing volatility throughout the world. Things are either happening faster than before or in directions not imagined before, or both. In fact, we expect "non-normal" things to happen with a higher degree of frequency than "normal" things. For example, our access to the global market has exceeded imagination. What used to take years to accomplish in the past, now takes just days or even minutes. As changes these days are often accompanied by speed and magnitude, as well as driven by different factors joined together by spaghetti junctions, we believe that volatility, scale, and complexity must go hand in hand.

Historically, volatility has been viewed as a problem or something to be avoided. We wanted to protect ourselves from volatility because it represents change, uncertainty, and discomfort. The frequency of events that occur outside the norm *are the norm*, and therefore volatility itself is the new norm. Exceptions are fast becoming rules.

Lately, we have seen a great deal of seismic shifts, which many people would describe as "black swans," otherwise known as large-scale events, which are unpredictable. They could be environmental, such as a tsunami or an earthquake, or terrorist acts that have gone down to an individual level (attacks with a truck or an ax). On a social level, Brexit and the US presidential election are the most visible black swans. Hence, we have added scale to volatility. In today's connected and high-tech world, small events have amplified impacts, and individual actions can escalate into global troubles.

Unpredictability implies new opportunities are possible. In the context of DRIVE, *V* could offer despair, a sense of loss and confusion, but in our view, it actually offers redemption. It allows us to step out of the terrifying trance of trying to fix things using the old models. We can move forward and construct a new model to fit the new paradigm. We can think in terms of what needs to be taught, of what is relevant today, and of what needs to be addressed.

V is where people can feel empowered to change their future by changing their *today*. Many of the things that happen in *D*, *R*, or *I* cannot easily be changed. The crimes have been committed and the damage is done, but *V* is where change is feasible. The only thing we know for certain is that if we don't do anything, we're in trouble. Our problems will only deepen and intensify and create more problems. *V* forces us to accept that what worked in the past no longer works in the present.

Traditionally, we used formulas and mathematical models to predict the future and measure risk. Ever since the development of science, we have entrusted ourselves to the reliability of numbers. As the world and how we live become ever-more complex, it is very difficult to quantify events. This is the reason why DRIVE is not backed up by quantitative analysis, in case the question popped in your mind.

Take finance, for instance. One of the most important concepts in corporate finance is the modern portfolio theory. It is a mathematical framework for assembling a portfolio of assets, such that the expected return is maximized for a given risk level. Industries have been built upon this observation. It is now an integral component of any business school finance curriculum.

Yet, there is a slight problem with this popular theory: it assumes that the market follows the bell curve—that the market works like a clock, as predicted by statistics. Nothing is further from the truth. As the world-renowned mathematician Benoit Mandelbrot notes:

> In fact, the bell curve fits reality very poorly. From 1916 to 2003, the daily index movements of the Dow Jones Industrial Average do not spread out on graph paper like a simple bell curve. The far edges flare too high: too many big changes. Theory suggests over that time, there should be fifty-eight days when the Dow moved more than 3.4%; in fact, there were 1,001. Theory predicts six days of index swings beyond 4.5%; in fact, there were 366. And index swings of more than 7% should come once every 300,000 years; in fact, the twentieth century saw forty-eight such days. Truly, a calamitous era that insists on flaunting all predictions. Or, perhaps, our assumptions are wrong.[1]

Therefore, the field of finance needs to develop a new algorithm to think about solving problems and inject some nonquantifiable elements into the mix. More black swans or not, the future is going to be more volatile and complex as a result of technological onslaughts, particularly with

---

1   Benoit B. Mandelbrot and Richard Hudson, *The (Mis)Behaviour of Markets: A Fractal View of Risk, Ruin and Reward* (London: Profile Books, 2008), 13.

the accelerated developments of robotics, algorithm, and artificial intelligence (AI).

Robots have always been science fiction stuff. But two recent breakthroughs have unleashed the long-awaited arrival of robotics.[2] The first is the creation of belief space, which is a mathematical framework that allows us to model a given environment statistically and develop probabilistic outcomes. For robots, modeling belief space opens the way for greater situational awareness. Until recently, it is far too complex and difficult to perform computations to achieve this, a task that is made more challenging by the limited sets of robot experience available to analyze. Yet, advances in data analytics have allowed for a breakthrough on this matter. This is reinforced by the second key development: cloud robotics. Linked to the cloud, robots are no longer confined to their own learning experience. They can now access vast amounts of data and shared experiences to enhance the understanding of their own belief space. Robots can simply "learn" quicker as a result.

Robots or algorithms[3] have started to be more systematically deployed. "Several years ago, we have been helping

---

2   Alec Ross, *The Industries of the Future: How the Next 10 Years of Innovation Will Transform Our Lives at Work and Home* (London: Simon & Schuster, 2016).

3   Through the interviews with senior executives, it is interesting to see that they were using robots and algorithms interchangeably. One may think that in both cases, it is about machines doing the work for humans.

companies to do BPO [business process outsourcing—offshoring operations to lower cost countries]. It was still the norm. These days, we are seeing more and more requests from clients setting up RPA or robotic process automation," said John Morley, a managing director at Accenture, a global professional services company.[4]

To many people, AI is pure science fiction. This may be the case for the so-called artificial general intelligence—those that are capable of carrying out any cognitive function like a human, have self-awareness and self-consciousness. Yet, artificial narrow intelligence or ordinary AI—those that follow orders or a set of instructions to carry out or improve itself in carrying out a certain task—is already everywhere. Every time you Google, you are engaging such AI. For most of us, a majority of the tasks that we perform each day can be broken down into four fundamental skills: looking, reading, writing, and integrating knowledge. AI has been helping with all these tasks in a wide range of situations, and its usefulness is spreading and deepening.[5] Three key developments have hastened its arrival: cheap parallel computation, big data, and better algorithms.[6]

---

4   Interview with John Morley, September 28, 2016.
5   Callum Chase, *Surviving AI: The Promise and Peril of Artificial Intelligence* (San Mateo, CA: Three Cs Publishing, 2015).
6   Kevin Kelly, *The Inevitable: Understanding the 12 Technological Forces That Will Shape Our Future* (New York: Viking, 2016).

V is a catalyst for some of the issues we examined in the first part of the DRIVE framework to become opportunities. If we can understand the language of economics through the lens of volatility, scale, and complexity, we can adapt much better. The shock that *V* presents also provides an incentive to do things differently. It's probably the most convincing and affirmative trend, because it allows people to move from contemplation to action.

We've heard students and colleagues be inspired enough to make the leap and say, "How can we change? How can we take a more experimental approach? What version of my idea is going to withstand the test of time?" These kinds of questions suggest a willingness to accept volatility, scale, and complexity as the new reality and create in accordance with those factors. *V* is almost like a springboard in which we transition from the immobility of *D*, *R*, and *I* toward conscious decision making that can unleash opportunities currently unnoticed.

THE BAD NEWS

V, in many ways, is a continuation of the discussion around inequalities. Machines used to eat up blue-collar jobs. This is not new. John F. Kennedy, in an interview back in 1963 said, "We have a combination of older workers who have been thrown out of work because of technology and younger people coming in . . . too many people are coming into the labor market and too many machines are throwing people out."[7]

Increased automation in the last five decades is contributing to the weakening of the middle class as robotics and automation continue to take away white-collar jobs. A recent report points out that there could be more than five million jobs lost to disruptive labor market changes between 2015 and 2020 worldwide, with a total loss of some seven million jobs—two-thirds of which are concentrated in routine white-collar office functions, such as office and administrative roles. Manufacturing and production roles would continue to decrease.[8]

Activities we thought would happen five years from now are already happening, such as the rise of machine learning, and things are happening at a much quicker pace. More and more people will be without jobs. Not only does this lead to high unemployment rates and the necessity for government intervention in the form of benefit payouts, but people without jobs also don't have money to spend. Yet, most developed economies today depend heavily on consumption for GDP growth. So, if no one is

---

7   John F. Kennedy interview by Walter Cronkite, September 3, 1963, https://www.youtube.com/watch?v=RsplVYbB7b8.
8   World Economic Forum, *The Future of Jobs Report* (Geneva: World Economic Forum, 2016).

spending money, or more precisely, only a few people have the money to spend, it will be difficult to sustain further economic activities. This, in turn, as one can imagine, could push producers out of business by deploying more automation to cut costs and maintain profitability, both of which further decrease the number of jobs and consumers.

It's not just about the loss of a paycheck or economic incomes; it's also about impeding social mobility. Many jobs in the service sectors, such as restaurants and retail, have been an important part of the career profile for a lot of people around the world. Young people, women, minorities, immigrants, and those with only high school qualifications very often depend on these jobs financially and use them as the first rung to climb the social ladder.

The middle earners are losing ground quickly, and the reasons are straightforward. One, more and more jobs traditionally held by these earners are vanishing. It is easy to imagine that rapid developments of AI and robotics would only accelerate their disappearance. Two, if increased productivity is the result of the deployment of technologies, there is no reason to pay human workers more.

A lesson from Economics 101 tells us that the three main factors of production are land, labor, and capital. Now, this concept has changed. In the increasingly digitized world, land has become less important as an input for production. Labor, on the other hand, in terms of manual power, has diminished as a factor of production. Indeed, as we have been discussing, even brainpower-driven labor is losing its value.

That leaves the third, capital. Unlike its two counterparts, it is becoming ever-more important, not least because research and development require a constant injection of capital. For example, successful tech entrepreneurs need capital to fund their ventures and experiments. In effect, like success breeds success, capital breeds capital. Yet a middle-income earner without any capital who loses his or her job is going to have a very hard time rebounding.

A question some of our colleagues ask is: "How high does technology's reach go?" Is the C-suite safe, or are they living on borrowed time, too? The executives are by no means safe! Terence was invited to act as the judge on a panel at a recent hack-a-thon run by a global investment bank. To his surprise, there were quite a few start-ups promoting new apps and programs that imitate the work of a CFO. These new software programs/apps help companies manage working capital by figuring out when they will run out of cash, showing them the loans available from different banks, as well as the interest rates that can get through the financial stretch. Not only do these programs forecast the financials, but they also provide solutions for the various scenarios.

Evidently, jobs that are process or efficiency driven will be the first to come under attack, yet even jobs that require specialized knowledge are threatened by technology. The resources exist for smaller companies and start-ups without financial expertise to get help. They no longer need to hire specialists. The new programs and technologies allow them to keep costs lean for as long as possible, using affordable software instead of hiring an expert.

People view the outcome of the rise of technology in one of three ways. One, we are all doomed. All of the jobs will be gone and there will be nothing left. Only the rich will survive and everyone else will be living in slums. We'll be living in a world straight out of the film *Elysium*.[9] Two, when the machines take over, we'll be free from doing work, and we can enjoy more leisure time. From the values and gains generated by the machines and robots, we can be paying ourselves dividends. One suggestion is that government could start paying the so-called universal basic income, an unconditional government payment given to all citizens as a supplement to or replacement for wages. Only in this case, human beings can live rather well just on the spoils of the machines.

---

9   http://www.imdb.com/title/tt1535108/

The third possible outcome sits somewhere between these two extreme scenarios. Some jobs would be gone. It is unlikely that many routine occupations will be taken over by machines, leaving human beings chasing fewer jobs that humans can excel better in. Yet, let's not forget that technologies have lifted many people out of abject poverty in various parts of the world. This is a trend that will continue. For those of us living in the more economically advanced societies, it is more difficult to imagine the new jobs that technologies will create than for us to place too much weight on the vanishing positions and too little weight on the ones about to be created.

THE GOOD NEWS

Given what we know, what is the future of employment and employability? In a world of ever-increasing automation, AI and robotics, how can humans make themselves valuable and employable?

One of the ways that we can limit and even harmonize the impact of technology on our jobs is to reflect on the very definition of labor. What does it mean? How can *we disrupt* it? Can labor be allocated to more creative or imaginative pursuits, where we utilize the artistic side of our brains, as opposed to the mechanical? The nature of labor needs to be reexamined in order to discover new opportunities.

We'll explore an example that hits close to home for us within the academic world. In the last few years, mass open online courses (MOOC) have become wildly popular. Professors record their classes and make them available online. Students from around the world now have direct access to pre-recorded classes in a variety of subjects, as well as the opportunity to have a remote classroom experience.

If universities start to utilize MOOC for fundamental core classes, there will be a lot of unemployed professors floating around. We're facing the same fate as the rest of the professional sector. However, opportunity lies within the threat of being taken over by technology. Those at-risk professors can work with companies or organizations in their respective fields on specialized action projects. This means working directly with companies to solve real-time issues by being more involved in research projects, publication creation, presentations, and conferences.

If we as professionals can evolve with technology, we have the opportunity to participate by being included in the conversation, instead of pushed out of it. No human being can win the war of cost effectiveness against a robot or automation, but we can find ways to enhance and contribute to its evolution without being sacrificed in the process. The fear surrounding increased automation and

AI only becomes a problem if we sit around passively and do nothing about it.

If we view volatility as an opportunity to increase our own productivity and value, we have a much better chance of survival. Volatility implies new events can be made possible, which can also mean new opportunities. A business or a business model that can handle big changes in the economic environment will certainly do better. Take the case of supermarkets and economic cycles. Conventional thinking dictates that grocers in general worry about recessionary periods as consumers would cut their spending. Yet, this is not always the case. "Here at Lidl, economic downturn doesn't necessarily bother us too much as we have gained new customers as a result," said Dirk Kahl, CFO of Lidl in the UK. He added, "When recession hits, like the one in 2008, many consumers would start buying from us, because we offer better prices to them. Yet, when the economy picks up again, they would not leave us. This is because when they started shopping with us, they found the value for money of our offerings to be rather high, so much so that they would stay with us even when they can shop elsewhere." [10]

Events like Brexit also help companies and bring new opportunities. Club Med, for example, specializes in

---
10 Interview with Dirk Kahl, September 22, 2016.

all-inclusive vacations at "vacation villages" in a number of (usually exotic) locations around the world. Vacation sales have gone *up* in the UK after the referendum. "With the uncertainty, more and more people want to spend less on goods and products but more on having a great experience and quality time with their loved ones. They see this as a better use of money," Estelle Giraudeau, UK managing director of the company, told us. She adds, "Life is tough, and people want to use their holidays as a way to bond family life to get through the uncertainty."[11]

It's in our best interest to adjust our definition of labor from one level of sophistication to another. The integration of physical, digital, and biological technology will profoundly alter the future. We can use the acceleration of volatility, complexity, and scale to achieve a greater impact.

The fact is, AI is already happening all around us in almost everything we do. Yes, it has replaced a lot of jobs, and yes, it will continue to do so, but it has also made our modern lives that much more convenient. AI will always be able to learn faster and do things more efficiently than humans, but we are very far away from the day when robots will be able to respond to a moral dilemma or make decisions.

---

11   Interview with Estelle Giraudeau, October 25, 2016.

Nevertheless, we're not doing ourselves any favors relying on outdated models. Our inherited, twentieth-century mindset sought symmetry, order, and structure. We tried to use mathematical models to have a better sense of control around decision making. The entire principle of risk management was centered in forecasting. We are facing a historical opportunity, right now, to create the future by using new, integrated models.

With volatility comes the necessity to examine events from multiple different disciplines. The goal is to see a more comprehensive picture and better navigate a world that can no longer be confined to a single analysis. For example, when companies make hiring decisions, they no longer look exclusively at the candidate's résumé and grade point average. That information can be integrated with additional perspectives, such as behavioral and social considerations. Is the candidate a millennial, a generation Z, or a baby boomer? What access have they had to the arts? How vibrant is their creative spirit? Those types of questions used to be excluded from a hiring analysis, but now they are a dynamic and necessary part of it.

We are matching qualitative and quantitative elements within the same process that we used to evaluate risk. That risk cannot be evaluated with the same assumption of control, but it can be evaluated as a proxy of something that *might* happen. The predictability has shifted from precise trajectories to broader cardinal points. Although we may have decided to go in a certain direction, other opportunities are likely to arise. Those opportunities may not be a part of our current landscape but could become so at a later date.

For example, established markets are bounded by geography or some other clear set of rules and parameters, which have much to do with physical location and geography. Predictability, in markets that have a clear boundary, clear rules, and customers to win, was the norm. Most business education from the 1980s onward was centered on the use of frameworks to determine expected behavior from firms, employees, and customers. But in a nonmarket strategy, the boundaries have been lifted, and the parameters are not controlled. We have to decide what direction to go based on our own unique set of variables. Reliance on predictability is not as plausible as in more conventional markets.

It is one thing to set the course from point A to point B, but what if there is a sudden storm? How will we adjust our plan for volatility? Our navigation from A to B will change trajectory over the course of time, but we will still arrive at our destination. We just have to use new skills to get there. If the old adage was about the plan and its backup, the new trend is toward perennial backup plans and beta versions, rather than clearly defined plans based on the science of expected outcome.

V is the primary shock that is disrupting the world from what it once was to what it will become. We can no longer be complacent, and we need to step out of our comfort zone. Handling the changes that volatility brings requires dexterity, flexibility, and versatility. The characteristics necessary are attributed to Leonardo da Vinci, widely regarded as somewhat of a polymath man. He was an individual capable of accomplishments across multiple spectrums—intellectual, artistic, social, and physical.

We need individuals who are capable of being entrepreneurial on many different fronts with sufficient knowledge of multiple disciplines. They need to be able to make decisions under ever-changing conditions. In short, we need modern-day Renaissance men and women at the helm—people who are empowered to make decisions even in the absence of data.

V is liberating because it allows us to focus on aspirations. All of the questions that surround this discussion are centered on the fundamental: What should we do? How can we harness change? What's coming down the road? What's the best route to our destination?

The disruptive impact of *V* insists that we look forward because looking back is no longer an option. It is one of the few trends in which we have the power to act. For example, the aging population does not necessarily have a direct impact on our choices, but volatility does. Best practices cannot be learned or copied anymore, which forces organizations to create their own stories. They must be agile so they can navigate the multiple layers of complexity and function in a fluctuating market.

Chaos is the norm, and it needs to be embraced as part of doing business. For example, if your business hits a slump, you're not necessarily going to lay off half of your staff. You recognize it as a normal business cycle and proceed without turning the ship around and heading back to the dock.

In the past, people were domesticated toward linearity. We expected things to follow a certain path, and if they didn't go the way we expected, we saw it as a sign of sure-fire trouble on the horizon. Whereas today, we need to be domesticated toward complexity, which is a richer playing field ripe with considerable opportunity.

TECHNOLOGY'S ROLE IN VOLATILITY, SCALE, AND COMPLEXITY

In 1965, Gordon Moore,[12] the founder of Intel, predicted that the number of transistors per square inch on integrated circuits had doubled every year since their invention. His observation is now referred to as Moore's law and was the first suggestion of continued exponential growth as related to technology. He thought it would last for a decade, but it lasted for four decades.

The law is probably coming to an end. There are actual physical limitations on how much capacity can go into a chip, and we have reached capacity.[13] New solutions to the space challenge are in the works, but so far, they are still in the early stages of development.[14] This means technology is not going to grow based on raw computing power alone. It will grow from a combination of other factors.[15]

For example, the advances we've seen since the rollout of the iPhone in 2007 have been incremental. The changes between the 4, 5, 6, and 7 have been gradual; nothing

---

12 http://www.intel.com/content/www/us/en/silicon-innovations/moores-law-technology.html
13 "More Moore: The Incredible Shrinking Transistor," *Economist*, http://www.economist.com/technology-quarterly/2016-03-12/after-moores-law#section-5.
14 "Quantum Computing: Harnessing Weirdness," *Economist*, http://www.economist.com/technology-quarterly/2016-03-12/after-moores-law#section-5.
15 Erik Brynjolfsson and Andrew McAfee, *The Second Machine Age: Work, Progress, and Prosperity in a Time of Brilliant Technologies* (New York: Norton, 2014).

really revolutionary is happening. They are just better iterations of the ones that came before. In all likelihood, what we will see from this point forward is technological growth from continued iterations on existing inventions. More importantly, even though they are just better iterations, they are doing more than laptops, despite the fact that laptops have far more computing power.

Combining cheap chips with cheap sensors allows us to do things we could never have done before. The science fiction from the 1920s is coming to life through robotics in large part because of connections to the cheap sensors. The good news is that anyone who is thinking about the future and how to improve it doesn't necessarily need the raw computer power alone.

For instance, while a certain amount of computing power is needed for graphics, the most important element in virtual reality gears is to have fast, accurate sensors to monitor where a user's head is pointing and not raw computing power. That way, the picture displayed by the goggles can be updated appropriately. If the sensors are inaccurate, the user will feel motion sickness. Having good sensors are more important than having superfast chips.[16]

---

16 "What Comes Next?: Horses for Courses," *Economist*, http://www.economist.com/technology-quarterly/2016-03-12/after-moores-law#section-5.

Hence, the future is likely to be about connecting the dots with the existing technology to create new breakthroughs (read: Internet of things). As computers become ever-more integrated into everyday life, the definition of progress will change. Computer companies are not going to slow down because the rise of computing power slows down; they will just find different ways to churn out products to make money. Technological development is likely to become less predictable, narrower, and less rapid than the industry has been used to. Combinations will play a much bigger role in our advancement.

The combinatorial evolution of technology has just started. For instance, WAZE—arguably the best traffic and navigation app available right now—is just the sum of a location sensor, data transmission through cell phones, a GPS system, and social networks.[17] Combining existing technologies in unique ways inform new business models, too. Uber is an example. It would not exist without credit card technology and GPS technology. Individually, those technologies are powerful; combined, they move mountains. Square is another great example of a combinational innovation. It requires a cell phone and an app to swipe a credit card. Suddenly, it is possible to receive and send payments from anywhere with a fraction of the investment it would have required to start from scratch.

---
17 Brynjolfsson and McAfee, *The Second Machine Age*.

Everybody can participate strategically through a high-velocity network. There used to be a cliché that emerging economies were only capable of copying technology, but that is no longer the case. Now, they are able to create it and compete on par with any other economy, world leader or not. The ability to digitize our economy is what makes scalability possible for everyone.

Take Mongolia, for example. It had the fastest growing economy in 2016, which was unexpected by so many. A few years ago, the country was suffering from the limbo generated by the disaggregation of the former Soviet Union and a suppressing presence of China in the region. By signing an agreement with the London Stock Exchange (LSE), Mongolia opened its resources to international investors who could propel growth. This was due to access to the latest market intelligence provided by the LSE, one of the most powerful stock exchanges in the world. The transformation was astounding; it was able to attract attention and investor interest thanks to the information technology system of a sophisticated Western player.

Before, we had to anchor many of our efforts in the physical resources available to us. For example, if we wanted to emulate the practices of a large tech company in the United States, we would need to replicate the operation with the same level of sophistication. However, the US market has more abundance in capital, resources, and investors than other places in the world. Our attempt at duplication would have had almost zero opportunity for true competition.

In today's digital landscape, we are seeing more and more innovations spring up from lesser known or under-monetized areas. The ability to replicate a business model or improve on an existing idea has been democratized through digital technology. Countries that are not well known for access to capital or resources are suddenly popping up on the global stage and going head-to-head with historically powerful giants.

With a little ingenuity, a wireless connection, and access to the right group of people, combination technologies are becoming the norm, just as volatility itself has. The ability to come up with breakthrough ideas is no longer exclusive to those who have money; now anyone can do it.

This is the most democratic process of knowledge distribution we have ever seen on a global level. We still have inequalities, but *V* is actually leveling the playing field in the technology sphere. Even countries that are on the lower end of the economic spectrum are capable of participating in the global economy. Technology has removed the barrier to entry.

The positive effects are already being felt in various industries throughout the world. For example, the health-care sector is now focused more on disease prevention than treatment. It is transforming from a sick-care industry to a well-care system. For one reason, prevention is much cheaper than treatment. This shift will favorably impact the problems we are seeing with the aging population and their impending health problems.

We have also seen tremendous breakthroughs in financial technology. The entire banking system as we know it is facing disruption. For the first time in history, banking access is available to a group of people who were traditionally considered "unbanked" or "underbanked," meaning they didn't have enough cash on hand to open an account or their credit was bad.

It's incredibly challenging to pay for anything—from a cup of coffee to rent—without a bank account or a credit card. For example, one of our students was from India. When he arrived in London, he could not open an account. He was turned away at every bank he tried. Eventually, he went to a financial technology (fintech) company and was able to open an account. He was finally able to live and work like everyone else in the country. Because of fintech, this student was able to participate in society, and thousands of others are as well. He was one of the luckier ones; at least he had the money to make a deposit. Compte-Nickel enables the unbanked in France to have an alternative bank account. For those with bad credit, Credit Karma helps individuals obtain free credit scores and search for the appropriate financial products. Challenger banks are set to make our financial lives better.

Access to technology has led to the expectation for wider participation. As a result, organizations are not making as much money on the sales of products. In economics, this is referred to as the marginal cost getting close to zero. With near-zero marginal cost models, organizations have to adapt and find new ways to create value. Many times, the product or service is given for free.

UberConference is a good example. With this technology, we have the ability to conduct lengthy, international conversations with multiple people around the world. All we need is access to Wi-Fi and a cell phone. Fifteen years ago, we would have had to pay the phone company at least $100 for the call. There was a binary relationship between the phone user and the company that provided the telephone connection. Now, that relationship is no longer necessary.

Given the new parameters, how does UberConference make money? It has to look for other means of making a profit than providing the phone connection. Usually, this is accomplished by offering "value-added" services, such as recording, transcribing, or call summaries. Many companies have switched to subscription-based fees instead of the old "use now, pay later" model. The more people they sign up for premium services, the better.

UberConference, and so many other companies like it, allow access to services and products many people would never have had access to before. These companies don't cater to the wealthy; they are for anyone who has access to the Internet. This is what we mean when we say that technology is allowing for greater democratization.

EDUCATION, SKILLS, AND EXPERIENCE

The educational system would benefit from applying the ideas behind volatility, scale, and complexity to the curriculum to better prepare our kids for the realities of today's and tomorrow's world. One of the main reasons that the school system is ineffective is because it is centered on the old concepts of symmetry, structure, order, and rationality.

It can be argued that our current educational structure is actually the first robotic system in existence. Our curriculum follows a factory line model. The classes are divided by subject, one teacher is assigned per topic, the students sit down and listen in silence to the subject expert, and they move from class to class in accordance with bells. Some schools even take it a step further and self-segregate according to gender. We are still following the same industrial model that was established in Victorian England. It is antiquated to the point of embarrassment, and it is designed to train an army of administrators, not a nation of innovators.

The necessity for accreditation in society is partially responsible for killing student creativity. The word alone implies a modus operandi, which doesn't give schools too much room to think outside of the box or experiment with what or how they teach.

Our school system needs to get with the times and modernize their approach. Can schools change fast enough to meet the demands of the future, and will they? If connecting the dots and harnessing the power of combinational technologies is the key to the future, what are we doing to train our kids in those disciplines?

Thankfully, some countries are starting to experiment with new methods. Kids are assigned "homework," but they are given time during the day to complete their assignments. When school is over, they can go home and play and be kids, without being bogged down with mountains of schoolwork. This new practice is contrary to the common belief that the only way for kids to get smarter is to make them work harder and longer. But it seems to be working.

If we want our kids to understand the realities of today's world, the schools need to mirror what is happening outside of the classrooms. There is an incredible opportunity to reinvigorate the curriculum and apply new teaching methods for enhanced learning.

For example, kids still sit down in the classroom and take notes the same way they did a hundred years ago. Research has shown that people learn more and process better when they are standing.[18] Also, children are still being evaluated on an individual level, but in real life, collaboration is what defines success.

Terence sat next to an expert in fintech at a recent event. He said his daughter had been very interested in building things, but over the years at school learning processes, she lost all interest in building. School curriculum, even at the university level, should be based on doing new things. It should concentrate on making children curious, rather than force-feeding them knowledge.

---

[18] https://www.sciencedaily.com/releases/2016/01/160114113635.htm

Educators need to stress creativity, which means kids should be encouraged to think outside the usual frame of reference. They need to connect the dots and have the confidence to speak up and think independently. Above all, they need to have the skills to communicate those ideas and convince others that what they are proposing is worth listening to.

Students, especially those at business schools, should be taught about the latest technologies. As Giraudeau told us, "The skills that managers need for tomorrow is not just managing people. They need to be able to manage both people and robots."[19] This implies that current business school curriculum is providing only half of what we need.

Technological advancements are hindering skill development. One of the greatest challenges facing professional service companies is enabling junior staff to accumulate experience. With algorithm and data analytics, an increasing amount of work is completed by machines. Knowing this, many clients have requested fee cuts by reducing the number of junior staff involved in an engagement.

While this is good news from the cost perspective, "it poses a huge problem to developing talent. If many of the junior roles are outsourced or replaced by technology,

---

19 Interview with Estelle Giraudeau, October 25, 2016.

fewer juniors will be required. And those juniors will not be exposed to some important learning situations, which would now be outsourced or replaced by technology. So if the client is reluctant to pay for juniors to be trained 'on the job' or to attend meetings, how can the next generation accumulate the necessary all-round skills and experience as their career develops? From the employer's perspective, there will also eventually be a smaller pool of junior talent from which to find the next generation of mid/senior professionals and leaders. When I was a junior, I picked up invaluable lifelong lessons by doing the basic tasks, learning on the job, and attending client meetings," said Gavin Weir, a partner at White and Case, a global law practice. "No amount of technology or theory training can replace real-life experience."[20]

As academics and parents, we are highly attuned to these opportunities. We see *V* as the greatest driver of actual change. Change is inspired not by an intellectual revolution but by the fact that our foundation is shifting. That sense of instability pushes people to seek new solutions, new models, and new ways of surviving and thriving in the evolving paradigm.

We asked Christophe Le Caillec, SVP and CFO of Global Consumer Services at American Express, what advice

---
20 Interview with Gavin Weir, November 15, 2016.

we should give to our children. He suggested that we tell them to "pick a global industry that can scale very quickly and try your luck. If it doesn't work, quit quickly, and try another player. Kids' ability to adapt quickly allows them to win in the future and quit very quickly. We, the older generation, keep telling them 'be patient; it is not a sprint. It's a marathon. Focus on the long term,' etc. This might be very bad advice! Millennials are well prepared to win in the future. The older generation should play more video games!"[21]

In a world that is characterized by volatility, scale, and complexity, the next generation will be prepared by keeping an open mind, having the right attitude, and being responsive to changes. Maybe, as Le Caillec advised, we should all play more video games.

---
21 Interview with Christophe Le Caillec, April 14, 2016.

CHAPTER 7

E: ENTERPRISING DYNAMICS

The fifth and final megatrend in the DRIVE framework is enterprising dynamics. Vast changes are occurring in how we do things and how commerce operates. The speed of change has not only given birth to new types of business, but also existing companies of all ages and sizes are thinking about their next steps all the time. As a result, there is an abundance of important new business models emerging today. The new models can be directly attributed to the phenomenon we have discussed in relation to *D*, *R*, *I*, and *V*.

At first, we thought *E* would stand for entrepreneurship. But we decided that it is inadequate to describe the reality.

People tend to associate the word *entrepreneurship* with start-ups and small and medium-sized businesses (SMEs). However, many large companies are constantly innovating as well. Many small businesses run more efficiently and effectively than corporations. To capture such spirit from businesses of all sizes, *E* stands for enterprising dynamics. Mark tends to call it emerging business models when he teaches DRIVE, mainly for the emerging nature of some of the practices that are changing the way markets and industries are evolving.

Technology, on its own, is not terribly interesting to the world at large. What is interesting and directly applicable to everyone is how technology is developed, applied, and relied on by both businesses and individuals. It allows us to continually come up with new ways to change society and the world for the better.

Rather than focusing on new technological advances or society in general, enterprising dynamics takes us back to our business roots. We will focus our discussion on some of the new business models that are emerging and share a few examples of companies that are using them effectively. Some of the companies are from countries that are not typically associated with innovation or breakthrough ideas.

Emerging economies are finding a place on the global economic stage, despite the fact they don't have the same access to resources as established economies. The so-called little guys are getting in the game because they have access to the information stream and the ability to communicate far and wide. Let us be clear. They may not be fully proficient in the cloud or part of the fledging platform that is called Internet of things, but the little guys are partially able to participate in the global economy with simple but distributed access to reliable technology, such as cell phones, text messaging, and increasing access to the Internet.

Economists used to reference the "north versus south" divide, but events and innovations within the last twenty years have flipped the coin. The epicenter has shifted from North America, Europe, and Japan to far-flung parts of the world.

V and *E* offer hope for all of those affected by the harsh realities of *D*, *R*, and *I*. The uprise of people in the southern and eastern parts of the world demonstrates that more countries are participating in the global economy. Integration is taking place on a much larger scale than ever before. We are now looking at the world through the new lens of "south versus north."

HOW OTHER COUNTRIES APPROACH INNOVATION

Former US Vice President Joe Biden once said, "China—and it's true—is graduating six to eight times as many scientists and engineers as we are. But I challenge you, name me one innovative project, one innovative change, or one innovative product that has come out of China."[1]

Carly Fiorina, the former Hewlett-Packard CEO and former Republican presidential candidate said, "I have been doing business in China for decades, and I will tell you that yeah, the Chinese can take a test, but what they can't do is innovate. They are not terribly imaginative. They're not entrepreneurial, they don't innovate, and that is why they are stealing our intellectual property."[2]

There is apparently confusion between the words *invention* and *innovation*. An invention is when something entirely new is brought into the market. Historical inventions are things such as electricity or the telephone. Innovation, on the other hand, is the act of coming up with new ways of doing things or variations. Invention and innovation are not mutually exclusive. There are several areas of the

---

1 http://politicalticker.blogs.cnn.com/2014/05/28/biden-name-one-innovative-product-from-china/
2 http://time.com/3897081/carly-fiorina-china-innovation/

world that have been overlooked because of confusion between the two terms.

For example, China is not widely recognized for invention, but its innovation accomplishments are off the charts. One example is WeChat, which is the Chinese version of WhatsApp, a messaging software. WeChat started as a clone of WhatsApp, but the Chinese market evolves differently than other markets. WeChat started to roll out new features that WhatsApp never developed, and today, it is an integration platform that combines instant messaging, Facebook, and Overtime. WeChat evolved with the market and surpassed the competition in sophistication and usability. It is so much more than an app; it has search functionality as well as mobile payment options, which is where it really took off. It's almost like a bank in your pocket. Very few people use cash in China anymore.

We were with a friend from China in Switzerland recently who was surprised when we needed to go to the machine to pay before going back to pick up the car. It costs way more to build and maintain the parking garage payment machines than it does to integrate payment into an app. Why do we still have to physically get out of the car and pay cash—in some cases, the exact amount—to park a car? How much does it cost to manufacture and ship those payment machines?

The smart way forward is to make things as fluid as possible. There are many areas, such as the parking garage payment system in the West, that simply have not caught up with the rest of the world. Perhaps it's because there is a lack of momentum or maybe there is resistance to change. Either way, we are being surpassed.

WeChat is precisely the kind of innovation that defines enterprising dynamics—new products or services that are not entirely original from the perspective of invention but are groundbreaking, nonetheless. We see this area as the greatest opportunity before us today, not just in emerging economies but in well-established economies as well.

Some people argue that China is still a closed economy. They say the government favors its own companies over others and won't allow foreign competition into the country. This is true on some level, but it doesn't mean there is nothing to learn from China and its innovations. Just as the north/south paradigm has shifted, so too has the old assumption that the East learns from the West.

The *Economist* recently ran an article that stated Western countries should pay close attention to what is happening in China and cited the WeChat business model as a specific example.[3] There needs to be greater emphasis on the East as an innovative technological hotbed. We should not simply focus on Google, Apple, Facebook, and Amazon (GAFA) but also Baidu, Alibaba, and Tencent (BAT). A recent study points out that Chinese companies are able to compete directly on science- and engineering-based innovations. They are exceling in those innovations that are based on efficiency and are customer focused.[4]

China isn't the only country making waves. Many other resource-limited countries are using frugal innovation, which is the process of reducing the cost and complexity of an idea, usually in production. It is the ability to come up with smart solutions to problems in the absence of resources. Frugal innovation isn't exclusive to any one country or region, although India is well regarded for a practice called Jugaad innovation,[5] which argues that the West must look to places like India, China, and Africa for a new bottom-up approach to innovation. New business models are emerging from everywhere, and we cannot afford to just ignore them.

There are hundreds of examples of frugal innovation, but

---

3   http://www.economist.com/news/business/21703428-chinas-wechat-shows-way-social-medias-future-wechats-world
4   McKinsey Global Institute (MGI), *The China Effect on Global Innovation* (N.p.: MGI, 2015).
5   http://jugaadinnovation.com/

our favorite is well documented. Some parts of rural India do not have electricity 24-7, and there are other parts that don't have it at all. In the absence of electricity, how do people keep their food fresh? Someone made the discovery that a box made out of clay keeps food just as fresh and for just as long as an electricity-fueled refrigerator. Of course, clay boxes don't cost as much to produce, there is not as much environmental waste, and it doesn't use a lot of resources.

Frugal innovation is centered on the practice of devising low-resource solutions. It starts with a dire need because as they say, necessity is the mother of all invention. When resources are tight—or nonexistent—creativity ensues. How can you make the most of what you've got? Over time, Jugaad innovation has become more mainstream. For example, Tata Motors in Mumbai reexamined the automobile manufacturing process. Using frugal innovation, it is able to sell cars for as low as $2,000. Tata embodies frugality by increasing efficiency using limited resources, assembling them together, and offering an inexpensive solution.

Another example is the French yogurt company Danone. With the goal of fighting world poverty, it opened a tiny manufacturing operation in Bangladesh to produce some of its yogurt, provide local people with jobs, and offer a nutritious food to the community.[6] From the outside, the factory doesn't look like much, but the company figured out a way to optimize the production flow and increase output at the same time. Its new methods were so successful from a cost-saving standpoint that it is now looking into how to better streamline its core production facilities in Europe. Danone's success came from taking a frugal approach, on top of a noble, poverty-fighting initiative.

Innovation is fueled by ingenuity. When something is lacking, what is the best way to capture some measure of it for use? We see ingenuity all around us. For example, a company in the United States called Rebound has developed an app to connect your phone's Short Message Service (SMS) to the Internet. If you are in the middle of nowhere, as we often are and cannot get a signal, the Resources app accesses Wi-Fi through SMS technology. It's not as effective as Wi-Fi, but it works. It offers a solution to a problem.

Also, there are regions in Peru with limited access to water. However, they do have high altitudes and humidity. Someone figured out a way to create water by collecting the humidity droplets on an advertising billboard high up in the mountains. Without giving up on the primary

---

6   http://www.danonecommunities.com/en/project/grameen-danone-food?mode=history

objective, he reinvented his approach to the problem of access to water.

Low-resource innovation shows the world what is possible. We should all learn to do more with less. Our society is material intensive, and we tend to gobble up our resources instead of protecting them and repurposing them. The whole idea of frugal innovation is to learn how to reduce the cost of doing things without compromising the quality or functionality of the product. If we can understand this and get behind it, we can integrate business models and mindsets from emerging economies into our society.

The word *innovation* is often associated with technology, but it really refers to simply doing things differently. Frugal innovation can happen anywhere. It is a system of process improvement. For instance, hospital visits are cheaper in India than they are in America. It's not because the care is inferior; it's because they are much better about approaching their problems creatively. They are organized more efficiently, transfer responsibilities to their staff, and set experimentation expectations.

On the contrary, we see instances of waste throughout the medical community in the United States. When you visit the doctor, the first thing he or she does before an examination is put on a pair of latex gloves. At the end of the appointment, the doctor removes the gloves and throws them away. That same doctor sees at least thirty people a day, which means he or she is throwing away a lot of latex gloves. Those gloves will never be used again, but the hospital has to pay for them. Latex gloves are a perfect example of a cost that could be minimized. What if there was a sterilization system so the gloves could be reused? Think of the money a system like that would save and how much waste would be reduced.

We are trapped in an imperialist model. We think our systems are perfectly adequate and there is no need for improvement. We've inherited the expectation of unlimited resources and gravitate toward a "bigger is better" mentality. Enterprising dynamics and the innovation we are seeing within it allow us to think more intelligently about redistribution of resources. By considering processes and challenging the status quo, we will be able to address at least some of the problems that communities face.

Since the financial crisis in 2008, we have been in a low-growth state. While some countries recovered, others have not and may never. Those who are still struggling have had to learn how to be extremely conservative with what they have. They are also more prudent when it comes to risk. In a low-growth model, low-cost innovation is the only way to uphold the GDP. Even at a macroeconomic level, frugal innovation is the best way to ensure prosperity.

Innovation is change: change in practice, change in approach, and change in mindset. The West doesn't have a monopoly on good ideas. A lot has happened since the Industrial Revolution in the eighteenth century. There are many new discoveries and innovations that go unnoticed. It's time for people to sit up and take notice of the changes going on all over the world, because there's a lot to learn, and we should learn from one another.

HOW BUSINESSES ARE EVOLVING

In response to many of the changes with innovation and technology, businesses must change, too. This is not to suggest that Western companies are standing still; everyone is looking for ways to get ahead of the curve, whatever that curve might be. Seismic shifts are occurring across industries to keep up with the pace of change.

These days, an increasing number of companies are more akin to technology integrators. We once spoke with a translation company, which told us that most of the translations are now completed by machines. It is only necessary to have a human translator look at the final version. Given that this company translates a lot of instructions and manuals as well as contracts for its commercial clients, it is far more important that its information technology (IT) system is seamlessly connected to those of the clients to ensure that everything runs as smoothly as possible. Effectively, it hires only a few translators but far more IT people.

Information companies are also moving toward the IT integrator model. "Since our company is now offering more and widening varieties of information to our clients to help them make decisions, we need to make sure that we receive, process, and disseminate data fast and accurately. This means that we have to ensure that our IT system is fully integrated and working flawlessly," said Mark Roomans, UK CEO of Morningstar, a global investment research and investment management firm.[7]

Business as a platform is seen to be an important consideration for many businesses, not least those in financial services. "To compete in the future, financial services companies will have to seriously consider opening themselves up via an effective API [application programming interface] strategy so they can take advantage of what many of the smaller fintech specialists can provide and offer, such as new services to their customers," says Susanne Chishti, CEO of FINTECH Circle, Europe's first

---

[7] Interview with Mark Roomans, November 14, 2016.

angel network focused on financial technology (fintech) opportunities, and coeditor of *The FINTECH Book*.[8]

The changes we are seeing demonstrate how businesses are evolving in response to the needs of the market. They are handling problems differently than they did before and harnessing technology to help with the transition. With little effort, great results are achieved.

As mentioned in the previous chapter, we are expecting more new technological innovations to come from the combination of existing technologies. Yet, innovation can also be gained from joining previously unconnected ideas together. New and useful ideas can come when technologies are paired with human concerns.

This is the idea behind Aumeo Audio, a start-up that is transforming the way we hear the world by customizing sound to each and every ear. "We discovered the idea behind Aumeo quite serendipitously," said Paul Lee, CEO and cofounder of the company. "My partner, Professor Andrew van Hasselt, a well-respected specialist in hearing, once talked to a patient who had been insisting on listening to a very specific song. At first, he was a bit perplexed. Later, he found out that particular song contains a lot of frequencies that complemented the patient's tinnitus,

---

8   Interview with Susanne Chishti, December 7, 2016.

hence giving her precious tinnitus relief. As it turned out, each person's hearing is unique, and all of us can benefit from tailored audio. This gave us the inspiration to tailor sounds for ears."[9]

Because Aumeo went through crowdfunding, Lee also shared another story with us. Some entrepreneurs are using crowdfunding as a low-cost—even potentially profitable—way to obtain real-world market feedback. Traditionally, companies that wanted to launch a new product or service poured their resources into surveys and focus groups. They raised the money to build a prototype and then tested it in the market. From there, they found a manufacturer and a distributor and raised even more money for production. They also paid to hold on to huge piles of inventory so they could be sold to the retailers. And then they pray that the product will sell.

Crowdfunding throws the entire traditional product launch process into reverse. It allows you to reach out to your market before you spend a dime creating the product. You can get real-time feedback on your concept. If people are interested, you can gauge exactly how much interest there is, and you can even get a commitment to buy (as buyers preordered). Because buyers paid you upfront, you can effectively use accounts payable for your

---
9 Interview with Paul Lee, December 22, 2016.

operation and production. The probability of success is much higher because the market has already been tested, vetted, and sold on the idea. Successful campaigns can even ride on the generated marketing buzz and use the success as proof to investors and retailers.

On the flip side, should the idea not fly, the team would still have built a community of would-be customers and received improvement ideas directly from the target audience. Worst case, even if the idea is deemed a failure, the resources lost would be limited to the crowdfunding campaign, sparing the team from producing and launching a product just to learn that it would fail.

Massdrop uses a similar concept but in a slightly different way. It offers a place where users discuss products they are interested in buying. The site then negotiates and organizes ordering the products, often obtaining group discounts in the process. This in itself is not a revolutionary concept. Several other companies, such as Groupon, have been doing this for a while.

Where Massdrop differs dramatically in one aspect is by doing crossovers with specific brands and manufacturers. The way this works is Massdrop will partner with a reputable, high-end product manufacturer, such as Fostex headphones. For instance, it sends out a message to all of its subscribers and announces a limited edition deal for 2,000 Fostex headphones. Anyone who is interested commits to buying the product by paying the full amount up front.

Fostex produces the headphones with the money the consumers have already spent to buy them, similar to the crowdfunding model. Fostex doesn't need to spend any money out of pocket, and it can predict—to the unit—the demand. If 1,500 customers are interested in buying, that's how many headphones Fostex produces. The inventory issue is erased; there are no problems with under- or overproduction.

So far, we are focusing on consumers paying businesses. What if consumers are enabled to pay one another? We think they would become more inclined to work with the known community than a faceless provider. Friendsurance, a peer-to-peer insurance company, is an example. The German company enables consumers to pull together and form a pot of money, from which payouts are made in case of accidents. One of the benefits is that participants will never pay more than the premium. In fact, they may get some of the premium back if there is no claim in that year. Another important key here is that the moral hazard issue is lowered. Because people pulled together, they can actually know one another, and there is less incentive to make an insurance claim.

Crowdfunding, Massdrop, and Friendsurance have just figured out how to apply technology in a smart way, and they are thinking outside of the box, which is what enterprising dynamics is.

HOW COMPANIES ARE APPROACHING PRODUCTS AND SERVICES

There are two major developments that will lead to new enterprises and increase such dynamics. First, today's new models allow businesses to identify their minimal viable product (MVP) with very little effort or investment. They can focus on the absolute least amount of work they need to do to get a market read on the product. From there, they can go through the various iterations and, over time, refine the idea. This means there is a much shorter time frame in which to come up with new products. The chances of success are much higher because you have the benefit of immediate market feedback. The trial-and-error component is key. You don't want to learn how to play golf in the dark. If you can't see where the ball is going, you'll never be able to adjust your swing so it lands correctly. You simply don't have the feedback to help you improve.

In the past, many technologies were available exclusively to people who could afford them, and the price point was high. Not everyone could buy a TV when it was first introduced to the public after World War II. Personal home computers were also prohibitively expensive at first.

These days, because companies are experimenting with MVP, many innovations are available to everyone at a low price. This is particularly true in the technology space, but organic food is another example. Although it's not readily available to everyone, there are more opportunities to buy organic than ever before. Slowly, organic food is becoming more mainstream, and consumers no longer need to go to specialty stores to buy organic products. There are now more choices.

THE NEXT BIG THING

The second major development in enterprising dynamics is blockchains. While the technology itself can fill an entire book, it is what the technologies can bring to society that speaks volumes. The central premise of this emerging technology is trust. Dubbed "the trust machine" by the *Economist*,[10] it is a breakthrough that holds the promise

---

10 http://www.economist.com/news/leaders/21677198-technology-behind-bitcoin-could-transform-how-economy-works-trust-machine

of reducing the cost of establishing and maintaining trust for both people and organizations.

"With this new trust protocol, individuals can exchange value by themselves in a secure setting without going through a third party or an intermediary. This has far-reaching consequence not just on financial services but also on the rest of the society. It is and will continue to create completely new business models, boost entrepreneurship, enable content originators to generate more value and will also change our relationships with the governments. Coupled with complexity economics, the blockchain can be used to gain a better understanding of markets and the effectiveness of monetary and fiscal policy. In fact, if used right, it can be the enabler of a new version of capitalism that is based on transparency and a higher level of mathematical exactitude," said Kary Bheemaiah, head of research at Uchange, a consulting company based in Paris, and the author of the book, *The Blockchain Alternative: Rethinking Macroeconomic Policy and Economic Theory*.[11]

Because the blockchain technology allows for genuine peer-to-peer trading with intermediaries, businesses that are based on the so-called aggregator model would be severely affected. Aggregators are those companies

---
[11] Interview with Kary Bheemaiah, November 16, 2016.

that use proprietary technologies to centralize supply and demand such as Uber and Airbnb. Even though they tend be called shared-economy companies, they have nothing to do with sharing. Airbnb does not share mattresses, and Uber drivers do not share their cars.[12] They make money by aggregating vacant rooms and driving services using proprietary platforms.

These platforms can be replaced with the adoption of the blockchain technology. Distributed application can allow for the creation of what is essentially a cooperative owned by its members. "Whereas most technologies have the tendency to automate workers on the periphery doing menial tasks, blockchains automate away the center. Instead of putting the taxi drivers out of a job, blockchains displace Uber to let 'everyone's private driver'[13] work with the customer directly."[14]

One of the defining characteristics of innovation is disruption. Companies need to build resilience into their daily operating procedures. Given the trajectory of innovation, disruption is only going to increase over time.

---

12 Alec Ross, *The Industries of the Future: How the Next 10 Years of Innovation Will Transform Our Lives at Work and Home* (London: Simon & Schuster, 2016).

13 This used to be the slogan of the company. Its current incarnation is, "Where lifestyle meets logistics."

14 Quoted in Don Tapscott and Alex Tapscott, *Blockchain Revolution: How the Technology behind Bitcoin Is Changing Money, Business and the World* (London: Portfolio Penguin, 2016).

Businesses are under siege on a regular basis from the constant stream of activity coming in from all directions.

Because enterprising dynamics unfold with the same characteristics as volatility, disruption is the new norm. The original disruptors will soon be disrupted. No one, not even the giants, can afford to be complacent. Just because some of these companies have reached the pinnacle, their spot at the top is not guaranteed.

If we understand that entitlement is not a part of the business vernacular anymore, we can raise a new generation of business leaders who are prepared to innovate accordingly. They will be able to make decisions with the awareness that the only constant variable in enterprising dynamics is disruption.

CONCLUSION

DRIVE is a systems-based perspective designed to help individuals and companies think about tomorrow and identify new growth opportunities today. The five megatrends within the framework—demographic and social changes; resource scarcity; inequalities; volatility, scale, and complexity; and enterprising dynamics—give us direction as to how the future will unfold.

It's important to look at the trends together in order to fully grasp the big picture. DRIVE is an invitation to a conversation about the global systems that link us all together. While *D*, *R*, and *I* may not be directly and immediately applicable to your business, the implications of them are still vital to understanding where we are going as a society.

The purpose of our society in the twentieth-century was growth. World War I, World War II, and the Great Depression were significant interruptions to the growth endeavor. Once those upheavals were behind us, peace and prosperity became the overriding model. Peace was the absence of war, and it became the norm, which is one of the great evolutions of society. We went from dying and starving to thriving and healthy.

What is the purpose of our society today? We created DRIVE to encourage people to ask questions. We want them to better understand how various elements are interfacing to define our current landscape. Individually, the trends don't tell us what direction we are headed as a society. Looking at the five megatrends together, on the other hand, do provide us with the full picture and tell us what type of society we are creating for the future generation.

Our parents lived in a world where they expected their children to do better than they did. We had the tools to bypass many of the challenges they faced as survivors of war and economic hardship. It was almost guaranteed that our generation would be more prosperous. Today, for the first time in history, we cannot guarantee that our children will do better than us. We already know the trajectories are not favorable.

Our motivation for DRIVE is the prosperity and health of the next generation. We want the same things for our kids that our parents wanted for us. What kind of world will they inherit because of our actions? How can we make better decisions to protect their future? The landscape they face is so vastly different than the one we see today. How can we best educate our kids to succeed professionally and be economically sustainable?

The best way we can help the next generation is by showing them how to think about where the world is going. We're not asking them to forecast the future. We are asking them to pay attention to what is going on around them. We want them to be aware of the various elements at play and how they are connected. What does the future look like if we do nothing today?

People in the business world tend to look at what is right in front of them and focus on the things that will immediately impact them. To that end, inequalities are not an urgent matter for everyone necessarily, although it is the biggest trend bomb we are sitting on. Even though "*I*" may not be directly relevant on a day-to-day basis in your business, it will have an impact on the social end of the spectrum. Few businesses will be able to thrive if society as a whole is deteriorating. Therefore, business owners need to pay attention to all of the underlying forces. They have the capability to mobilize resources and create better societies, and it is in their best interests to do so. Their own survival is at stake.

Policy makers in government should also be using the DRIVE framework to evaluate society's needs. They hold the key to shaping policies that can encourage not just businesses to consider the social implications of their actions but individuals as well. We all have the potential to achieve big change. Sometimes, all it takes is a little nudge to get the ball rolling.

What type of push is necessary for policy makers to take steps toward improving the health of our society? The best course forward is to examine the megatrends in the context of the immediate problems. The trends are not silos but rather one coherent, all-encompassing whole.

As educators, our primary focus is on teaching people how to think. Thinking is not a commercial endeavor, which is why it can be challenging to get people to focus on this topic. DRIVE is intended to be used as a way for organizations to engage in the big questions. We are trying to create sufficient awareness on why embracing megatrends is important for any entity. These discussions are not exclusive to analysts who are looking at risk; everyone needs to be exposed to what is currently happening.

DRIVE is also a vehicle through which people can discuss and argue the emergence of new trends with the understanding of what they mean for the bigger picture. It is a feedback mechanism whereby if something happens, it can be filtered and understood through the framework.

DRIVE is not an invention; it is a frugal innovation, born from our own limited resources. We haven't created anything new. We observed and modified what was already out there. Far from being a comprehensive tool, DRIVE is a means of interpreting reality according to the five major points of observation. It is not the car; it is the GPS system. Instead of just turning on the cruise control and hoping you get to where you want to go, DRIVE helps us to be active drivers on the road of life and pay attention to what lies ahead. Grab your keys and get in the car. The future is just around the bend. Which road will you take?

ABOUT THE AUTHORS

DR. TERENCE TSE (@TERENCECMTSE)

Alongside his ongoing advisory activities with supranational organizations, Terence regularly provides commentaries on the latest current affairs and market developments for the Financial Times, the Guardian, the Economist, CNBC, the World Economic Forum, and the Harvard Business Review blogs. He has appeared on radio and television shows on China Central Television (CCTV), Channel 2 in Greece, France 24, and NHK. Terence has also been invited to speak at the United Nations, the International Monetary Fund, and the International Trade Centre, as well as events in India, Norway, and the United Kingdom.

Terence is an associate professor of finance at the London campus of ESCP Europe Business School, the oldest business school in the world. He is head of Competitiveness Studies at i7 Institute for Innovation and Competitiveness, an academic think tank based in Paris and London. He is also a fellow at the Judge Business School, University of Cambridge.

Before joining academia, Terence worked in mergers and acquisitions at Schroders, Citibank, and Lazard in Montréal and New York. He also worked in London as a consultant at Ernst & Young focusing on UK financial services. He obtained his doctoral degree from the Judge Business School, University of Cambridge.

DR. MARK ESPOSITO (@EXP_MARK)

Mark is a socioeconomic strategist who has consulted in the areas of corporate sustainability, economic complexity, circular economy, and competitiveness worldwide, including advising to, among others, the United Nations Global Compact, national banks, governments, the European Parliament, NATO-wide Executive Development Programs, and municipalities in Massachusetts. He holds fellowships with the Social Progress Imperative and the Global Federation of Competitiveness Councils in Washington, DC, as well as the Mohammed Bin Rashid School of Government in the United Arab Emirates. Mark is also a Member of the Circular Economy Initiative at the World Economic Forum in Geneva.

Mark was appointed to Harvard University's Division of Continuing Education in 2011, where he teaches courses in Economic Strategy and Competitiveness. He also serves as Institutes Council Co-Leader for the Microeconomics of Competitiveness program at the Institute of Strategy and Competitiveness, Harvard Business School, led by Professor Michael Porter. Alongside his role at Harvard, Mark is a full professor at Grenoble School of Management as well as Hult International Business School and a fellow at the Judge Business School, University of Cambridge. He obtained his PhD from the International School of Management in Paris and New York and is candidate to an executive doctoral degree at École des Ponts ParisTech. He was inducted into Thinkers50 Radar in 2016.